# Bound-for-College Guidebook

# Bound-for-College Guidebook

## A Step-by-Step Guide to Finding and Applying to Colleges

*3rd Edition*

Frank Burtnett

ROWMAN & LITTLEFIELD
*Lanham • Boulder • New York • London*

Published by Rowman & Littlefield
An imprint of The Rowman & Littlefield Publish  g Group, Inc.
4501 Forbes Boulevard, Suite 200, Lanham, Mar  and 20706
www.rowman.com

86-90 Paul Street, London EC2A 4NE, United K  gdom

British Library Cataloguing in Publication Inform  tion Available

**Library of Congress Cataloging-in-Publication  Data**

Names: Burtnett, Frank, 1940- author.
Title: Bound-for-college guidebook : a step-by-st  guide to finding and applying to
  colleges / Frank Burtnett.
Description: Third edition. | Lanham : Rowman   Littlefield Publishing Group, [2022]
  | Includes bibliographical references and index  Summary: "From exploration to
  enrollment, everything the student needs to kn  and successfully navigate the high
  school to college transition"—Provided by pul  sher.
Identifiers: LCCN 2021060026 (print) | LCCN 2  1060027 (ebook) | ISBN
  9781475861815 (cloth) | ISBN 978147586182  (epub)
Subjects: LCSH: College student orientation—U  ed States—Handbooks, manuals, etc.
  | Universities and colleges—Admission--Hand  oks, manuals, etc.
Classification: LCC LB2343.32 .B88 2022 (prin  | LCC LB2343.32  (ebook) | DDC
  378.1/98—dc23
LC record available at https://lccn.loc.gov/20210  026
LC ebook record available at https://lccn.loc.gov  )21060027

*Dedicated to Jack, Alexandra, and Will.*
*Limitless educational and career opportunities lie before you.*
*Dream big dreams and then work hard to achieve them.*

# Contents

# Student Exercises

# Acknowledgments

As with the earlier editions of the *Bound-for-College Guidebook,* I must acknowledge the wisdom and knowledge of the many educators with whom I have interacted over my career. Of this extensive group, Rusty Shunk, retired Executive Vice President and Dean of Dickinson College, stands out as one that I have turned to regularly when I wanted to view the larger picture and see it through the higher education lens. My thanks to him and the dozens of nameless colleagues and friends who have influenced my words.

In addition, considerable information contained in this edition of the *Bound-for-College Guidebook* was contributed by three extremely talented students in the graduate program in counseling at Marymount University in Arlington, Virginia. Charlotte Morris and Savannah Noah did outstanding work in researching current trends in the admission practices and protocols that colleges are using today. Further, Courtney Bennett's work in the identification of student and parent resources made this a far better edition. I am indebted to each of them and wish them well in their future careers as professional counselors.

# Introduction

The *Bound-for-College Guidebook* contains much of the information the student who is navigating the high school to college transition needs to consider during this very challenging time in his or her life. Like in the earlier editions, readers will find guidance and information about the self-awareness, exploration, and decision-making strategies that should be mastered as they approach the preparation of their applications for admission and financial aid and experience the transitions of moving from K-12 to postsecondary education. Each chapter is designed to personalize the process and educate you in becoming a better explorer, decision maker, and applicant. Understanding this information will empower you throughout the transitional process you are going to be experiencing personally.

This edition takes the pulse of the current admission and financial aid climate by examining how information is created, stored, exchanged, accessed, and used by students and the colleges themselves during our ongoing technological revolution. In addition, an attempt has been made here to assess the impact which the coronavirus pandemic has and will continue to have on the way institutions conduct their affairs. Finally, this edition of the *Bound-for-College Guidebook* will examine the Varsity Blues Scandal that surfaced in 2019 and thrust a host of criminal acts involving illegal and inappropriate admission practices by parents, private agents, coaches, and athletic personnel into the public eye and resulted in many convictions of the wrongdoers.

Interspersed throughout the guidebook, the student will find a series of personal exercises. You will be asked to engage in personal assessment, answer questions, identify characteristics, and evaluate information that will help in the selection of your future college or university.

The product of the exercises will first be a profile of you—the future college student as seen through the characteristics that you are looking for in your future college. A by-product of completing the various exercises is a structure it will give to your personal transition from high school to college.

There are no right or wrong answers—sin ly your views, your choices, and how you think your future college experie e will help you realize your edu cational and career goals. At the complet n of all or most of the exercises you will possess a personal portfolio to gu le you through these times.

The guidebook also contains approxim ely one hundred of the most fre quently asked student questions (FAQs) ɛ out college admission and finan cial aid. Many are questions you have a ady raised and others represent concerns that haven't arrived on your pers al radar screen yet. They are the questions that counselors and admission ɛ l financial aid professionals deal with every day and each has been answered here for you. Knowing all or most of the answers will allow you to personali the whole process even more.

The process of college exploration anc lecision making is an evolution ary one. It will be influenced by your pe nal growth and maturation. The process will also be affected by the inforn ion you acquire and the ongoing experiences you have as a student. There re, the responses that you record here reflect a point in the process and sho ld be reviewed and updated sev eral times before you begin the serious ta of submitting college admission applications.

Ask the people that know you (parent, ounselor, teacher, or best friend) to review the student exercises you comp e in this guidebook from time to time. The more they know about the value ou place on the various selection criteria and the direction you are moving with your exploration, the better they will be able to guide and support you.

Your command of the information in e Bound-for-College Guidebook and completion of the various exercises wi allow you to put the colleges you are considering to a personal test. From wh you learn, you will be in a stron ger position to make decisions about whe to apply and where to enroll if admitted. You will also bring organization nd order to your personal search, decision-making, and application activitie

*Chapter 1*

# How Colleges Admit Students

## *Anatomy of an Admission Decision*

Admission officers are charged with the responsibility of selecting students who will meet the challenges of the college or university classroom while contributing to the academic, cultural, and social climate of the institution. Different institutions place varying emphases on the criteria they employ to admit students, but the vast majority of colleges consider all or most of the following factors.

### ACHIEVEMENT IN COLLEGE PREPARATORY STUDIES

A strong academic record in challenging courses throughout the high school experience will be the factor most likely to influence an admission decision in your favor. Your cumulative grade point average (GPA) and class rank (if computed by your school) will be viewed in light of the breadth and difficulty of the courses on your transcript and regarded as the best predictor of the kind of success you are likely to have in college. Colleges and universities have discovered a direct relationship between success in college and success in high school and they want to admit those students who have had positive experiences in the classroom.

### ACT, SAT, AND RELATED TEST SCORES

As a rule, admission test scores alone are not likely to result in either your acceptance or rejection. That is even truer today as many colleges and universities have either stopped requiring these test scores or adopted a "test optional" status. Students applying to any of the nearly two dozen institutions included in the California State University ystem, for example, should know that the system dropped test scores as an mission requirement.

Admission officers tend to view scores s a "snapshot" of the more complete person. Some large universities use t scores to reduce large numbers of applications down to a manageable nu ber for a more thorough review. Test scores may also be used for placement some classes or to award college credit for coursework considered the equi lent of the college experience.

## EXTRACURRICULAR ACTIVI IES, VOLUNTEERISM, SERVICE LEARNIN( AND WORK

These experiences present a picture of the udent outside of the classroom, a facet of the individual that is very importa to some colleges. Activities that involve an extension of an academic end vor (e.g., writing for the school paper) are often viewed more positively han those that are purely recreational or social (e.g., drill team). Today, n ny students are volunteering their time to people-oriented community proje s. Referenced more formally in some schools as "service learning," these xperiences are positively viewed by colleges. Involvement in some extracu cular activity is important.

## TEACHER AND COUNSELOR ECOMMENDATIONS

These firsthand observations by educators ho have worked with you during your high school experience can go a long ay in emphasizing your abilities, aptitudes, and interests. Formal recomme lations often allow the writer to present information about your personalit motivation for learning, or personal philosophy that may not become kn vn in any other way.

## ESSAYS AND WRIT JG SAMPLE

The colleges that require a student essay onsider this creative work to be an important ingredient in their admissioi lecision. Good admission essays result from careful planning and you mu allow adequate time for writing and editing. As the writing of an essay ca be a time-consuming task, this is one endeavor that needs to be integrated ir the larger calendar of admission activities.

## INTERVIEW

Some colleges require or recommend a personal interview, many which are conducted today electronically via Zoom, Skype and other digital communication systems. The staff member or alumni representative conducting the interview will prepare a report that becomes an official part of the admission folder. Successful interviews require that you be yourself and display genuine interest in the college. Interviews allow the applicant to bring up and place information into consideration by the college that is not necessarily addressed in the more structured application form.

## SPECIAL TALENTS AND CHARACTERISTICS

Any particular talent (e.g., athletic, dramatic, musical) that you have can be influential in your gaining admission to a college. You will need, however, to showcase or present those special skills to the professors, coaches, or admission officers responsible for evaluating your talents. A portfolio of your artwork or a video/audio tape of outstanding performances is often used to present these talents.

Colleges may also give added consideration to members of a particular group (such as underserved and underrepresented populations), children of alumni, or individuals with other unique characteristics they hope to attract.

## ARE COLLEGES LOOKING INTO NEW ADMISSION ASSESSMENTS?

Colleges and universities, especially the more selective ones, are beginning to look beyond the traditional criteria (e.g., grade reports, admission test scores, etc.) and explore new ways of screening and admitting applicants using "noncognitive" assessments.

Will students of tomorrow be asked to present a portfolio of their academic work and submit to a closer examination of their overall abilities, aptitudes, interests, and personal goals? If, in doing so, the college can strengthen its ability to admit students who will be successful, expect some such form of "noncognitive" assessment to be blended with the traditional techniques. The day when a majority of colleges move to this form of admission assessment is pretty far in the future, but certain elements may come sooner than you think.

The college or university may consider any or all of these criteria in making its admission decision. Just how much weight will be placed on a particular factor will vary from college to college. Ask an admission counselor at the colleges you're interested in attending to tell you how they make their decisions. Obtain a first year class profile and compare your more quantifiable features (e.g., GPA, test scores with those of admitted students. Remember, too, factors such as demographics, number of applications, and other things totally outside your control may be influential in the college's decision making.

## A JOURNEY BEGINS

In the college admission process, you get to decide where to explore, where to apply, and where to enroll if you are accepted. The college decides who gets in. Start out by knowing what you can control and do everything in your power to make the process work on your behalf. Be flexible. Hang on to your values, ideals, and sense of humor. A gigantic, new journey is about to begin.

## FREQUENTLY ASKED QUESTIONS

**Question:** Recently I read that a school district was seeking to improve the "college and career readiness" of its students. What does this mean?
**Answer:** Educators and policy makers are creating college and career readiness programs that are aimed at closing the gaps between the student and their ability to succeed at the next level, be it college or the workplace. College readiness speaks to how prepared the student is to take on the academic, psychological, and social challenges of the college or university experience.

Career readiness, on the other hand, addresses how well each student is equipped to secure a place in the workforce after high school or college—how suitable their knowledge and skills are in making them employable after graduation. The U.S. Department of Education, the National Governor's Association, and other national, state and local organizations have placed college and career readiness high on their respective agendas.

**Question:** Is it true that some colleges will disregard my high school's grade point average (GPA) calculation and create their own?
**Answer:** It's been known to happen. Many of the more selective colleges have their own criteria and formula for calculating the GPA, something they will do once they have your official transcript in hand. Less competitive institutions are more likely to use the school-generated GPA.

**Question:** I have heard conflicting reports about how tough it is to get into college now. Just what is the competition like?

**Answer:** The competition for getting into colleges comes from a lot of different places. Factors such as population growth, the rise in the number of high school graduates, a greater percentage of graduates wanting to go to college, and the number of applications filed by individual applicants can individually and collectively affect the admission competition in a given year. College costs and the availability of financial aid have also caused students to "shop around" more than they once did. One thing has not changed: competition at selective institutions remains high and admission to these institutions will be granted to those presenting the strongest academic and personal qualifications.

The total undergraduate (four-year and two-year) enrollment at degree-granting institutions has been on the increase for several decades, a rise that is expected to continue in the foreseeable future. The higher education community is still waiting to see what, if any, lasting impact the coronavirus pandemic will have on college enrollment. Every demographic indicator leads experts to a very simple conclusion—competition for college is extremely keen at present and will continue this way for some time.

**Question:** How do population shifts in the United States affect the enrollment at the nation's colleges and universities?

**Answer:** Very dramatically. When births go up, the number of prospective college-bound students rises proportionately—even though it takes eighteen or more years for those newborns to reach the college campus. As more students earn their high school diploma, the number seeking to go on to postsecondary education increases as well. In reverse, global events like the coronavirus and major economic recessions tend to thwart or temporarily slow enrollment growth. Other factors, like rising immigration numbers and additional international applicants, have also added to the pool of prospective college-bound students. Each of these factors has the potential to increase competition for every available college desk and every dorm room.

**Question:** My school does not calculate class rank. Will this affect my chances of admission?

**Answer:** Many high schools have moved away from the policy of calculating class rank for their students and colleges have found ways of adjusting to not receiving this information. If you attend a high school that is reasonably well known by the admission officers examining your application, they will understand how your achievement compares to your fellow students and will find some method of factoring this information into their admission decision.

**Question:** I've been receiving unsolicited applications and information from a number of colleges. Does this mean they are really interested in me?

**Answer:** In these days of direct mail marketing, Internet-driven communication tools, and social media sites, many colleges and universities are continuously engaged in major information dissemination campaigns. In addition, don't be surprised that your name might be included along with thousands of other high school students in the mass mailing lists (mail and electronic) that can be purchased by colleges. Just because you receive an unsolicited letter, viewbook, or application from a college do not assume that you are on a special list of desirable candidates. You will still need to meet the academic and personal qualifications of the institution.

**Question:** To what extent are colleges interested in extracurricular activities and work experience?

**Answer:** Numerous studies of how colleges make admission decisions indicate that they look first to your current academic achievement, admission test scores (if required or submitted voluntarily), evidence of your past school performance, and potential ability to do college work. While academic credentials are the primary factors in admission, the student's involvement in activities outside the classroom can be a significant supporting factor as well. Mere membership is not important enough. It is better to show a significant level of participation or leadership in a few activities than to be superficially associated with many. Some colleges like to see extracurricular activities that are an extension of the classroom experience (e.g., science fair, debate club, etc.).

**Question:** My dad said that getting into a good college is nothing more than a giant "roll of the dice" in which the student has little or no control. Is he right?

**Answer:** Highly competitive colleges accept one student for every seven, eight, or sometimes more that apply. In that sense, the odds in favor of admission appear very competitive. You must conduct a study of the colleges where your abilities, achievements, interests, and related criteria are competitive with the students they are admitting. Let's call what you learn your AQ—your "admissibility quotient."

Along the way, many students are denied admission to colleges and universities, an action they don't understand or have a hard time accepting. For this reason, every applicant should begin by matching his or her qualifications with the profile of the student the college or university is admitting. This single step can often get the pendulum moving in your favor. This is where you get to exercise control by applying to colleges that are likely to accept you. Your father's reference, however, to a "good" college is somewhat troubling. There are lots of good colleges and if you look hard enough, you will discover them.

**Question:** The valedictorian at my school was denied admission by a prestigious college that admitted another student from our class who had lower grades. How can this happen?

**Answer:** It usually means that the college is looking for students who have something more than a high GPA to present with their application for admission. Scholarship is an incredibly important factor in college admission, but scholarship alone will not open every admission door if the college is looking for other characteristics in its incoming first year class.

**Question:** I attend a high school that has an extremely rigorous grading system. Will colleges take that into account when reviewing my transcript and application?

**Answer:** Colleges know more than you think about the high schools that send them students. While they cannot be accused of having spies in your classrooms, admission officers, especially those at the more competitive colleges, make it their business to know things such as the rigor of a particular high school's academic coursework and the precision of the school's grading system. Further, the more students from your high school that attend a particular college, the better that institution knows of the ability of your peers to succeed at the collegiate level.

You should also know that your high school produces an annual profile to keep colleges current about grading systems, course offerings, and related information. This profile is often attached to the transcript that is forwarded in support of your application, especially if you have applied to a college outside your geographical region or the high school has not sent students to the college recently. Ask your counselor for a copy of the current profile.

**Question:** The media has been reporting that colleges have altered their admission requirements to meet diversity objectives. How will this affect my application?

**Answer:** Many colleges have programs in place to ensure that their institution attracts and educates a student body that is diverse, inclusive, and representative. These programs also correct past practices when members of minority groups, certain religions, women, and those from lower socioeconomic circumstances were either denied admission or were limited in their ability to access a full range of postsecondary education opportunities because of discrimination or financial circumstances. As a result, certain individuals and groups have been identified as underserved and underrepresented, and many colleges have targeted them in their diversity and inclusion efforts.

If your application is highly competitive you probably will not be affected in any way. If your academic abilities and chievements are less formidable, you are likely to face stiffer competition f  admission. Keep in mind, however, that many competitive colleges wi  accept most of their "realistic" applicants.

**Question:** Is it true that great grades in le  challenging high school courses will work against me?

**Answer:** Great grades will never work a  inst you. However, great grades in a sustained program of precollegiate co  ses are going to look even better. The more challenging the courses you tak  the more influence your overall GPA will have on those making the admis  n decision. Consistent with your abilities, use every opportunity to select t  more demanding courses. They will help you in two ways. First, they lool  great on your transcript, and second, the experience will prepare you for  e more rigorous academic work you will encounter in college.

**Question:** Is earning a degree on the Inte  et via distance learning a viable alternative for a student today?

**Answer:** The last twenty years or more h  e witnessed an explosion in distance learning options, ranging from the  portunity to earn a full degree to taking an occasional course or two online  Before the coronavirus pandemic sent the entire educational world into a dis  nce education or remote learning mode of some sort, the U.S. Department o  ducation was reporting that 37% of college students were taking one or mo  distance learning class and 18% were studying online exclusively. As soc  distancing became the order of the day those percentages went through t  ceiling. Now that almost every college is experienced in distance learnin  and students have had multiple exposures, it's certain that distance learn  g is here to stay. Consult with colleges of interest to determine the deg  e to which remote learning is a requirement or an option.

Distance learning has opened doors like  cheduling flexibility and promoting access to learning that may have been  erwise denied. Some institutions are even banding together to offer Massiv  Open Online Courses (MOOCs) that expand study access to a global audi  ce of students. On the negative side, the full opportunity for interaction b  ween and among faculty and fellow students, for example, is limited and  e social and cultural benefits of being a part of a college community are  ost. Online education works for some, but not for others. One thing, how  ver, is certain. Classes won't be cancelled because of bad weather.

**Question:** Can I expect to be treated fairl  n the college admission process?

**Answer:** Members of the National Association for College Admission Counseling subscribe to that organization's Statement of Principles of Good Practice: NACAC's Code of Ethics and Professional Practices, a document that recommends the fair and ethical treatment of students engaged in the high school to college transition.

Will you understand everything that is happening to you and feel that you have been treated fairly? In some instances, the answer is "no." Students denied admission to a college they really want to attend are hurt and frustrated by what they feel the college did to them. That is why it is very important to conduct a thorough investigation and discover the multiple "right" colleges for you. Don't allow your future education to be left to chance or narrow vision.

**Question:** It seems that more and more students are taking a "gap year" between high school and college. How does this work and is it the right thing to do?

**Answer:** The rising number of requests by admitted students to defer enrollment or take a "gap year" validate the popularity of this behavior. Some students want to work and help contribute to their college expenses, travel, engage in a service-learning project, or simply take a break. When the coronavirus pandemic entered the picture in 2020 many admitted students asked to defer enrollment as a health precaution and to wait for in-person learning to fully return. This student behavior led to signficant enrollment declines at some colleges.

For whatever reason, the student does exactly what she or he would do to gain admission to college. Upon receiving a letter of acceptance, the student requests an enrollment deferral stating a desire for a "gap year." Colleges and universities across the nation have reported receiving and approving such requests.

**Question:** Is there any way to learn in advance just how colleges make their admission decisions?

**Answer:** Telling you exactly how they make an admission decision would be like telling you the secret recipe. It might happen—but it probably won't. Good questions, however, can provide certain insights. If you have a particular question, pose it to an admission officer or counselor. Another, somewhat trickier way to look at how colleges make admission decisions is to examine the most recent first year class profile for the institution. Most profiles are published and accessible by contacting the admission office. How do you compare with recent enrollees? Remember that college admission formulas are constantly in flux due to changing demographics, curricular innovations, and related factors. The best way to get tl    answer to your question is to be direct. Ask!

**Question:** How have college costs and    ıdent borrowing led to students being identified as underserved and under    presented?
**Answer:** College affordability can never l    dismissed as an influence in the college exploration and decision-making    ocess and the ability to pay can often be traced to the "have and have not'    lichotomy that exists in our society. Even before the coronavirus pandemic    ıad its negative economic impact on the ability of many students and famil    s to withstand the impact of college colleges, many institutions were wre    ing with how to serve and make college more affordable for those not repr    ented because of cost.

These same institutions and others w    e also influenced by the media headlines citing the amount of debt incu    ed by student borrowers. Many institutions gave "ability to pay" a larger c    ısideration in their admission and financial aid policies as a result. Similarly,    ıe fair and equitable treatment of all applicants that was brought into questio    by the Varsity Blues Scandal saw many institutions review all admission and    nancial aid policies and practices and make changes where warranted.

*Chapter 2*

# College Exploration

## *Getting Off on the Right Foot*

The student has an incredible amount of control in the college choice process, a factor that is not understood by some and not acted upon by others. A veteran admission officer once remarked that there are ultimately four decisions made in the college selection process, and the student gets to make three of them. The choice of where to explore, where to apply, and where to enroll, if accepted, are in the hands of the student. The college decides what students it wishes to admit.

The future college student must respect the power that he or she possesses in the selection process and use it wisely in order to ensure the desired outcome. Timing is a critical factor in gaining and maintaining control over the admission process. By starting early, allocating appropriate attention to all of the information-gathering, decision-making, and application-filing tasks, the student is exercising the type of control that will produce the best results.

If there is a preamble to the college selection process, it is that there is no single "right" college for you—there are many. Avoid the anguish of trying to discover "the" college that is right for you. Effective exploration will unearth more than one. With that bit of philosophical guidance, consider the following as you begin to explore the educational opportunities before you.

### ACADEMIC FIT

Since institutions differ in the scholastic requirements they make of their students, you will want to look for colleges that "fit" you well academically. Fit means being challenged and being able to meet that challenge. Don't place yourself in an academic environment where you will simply coast for four years, and don't sentence yourself to constant pressure about whether you're going to succeed. Academic fit should be paramount in the selection of a college.

## ENVIRONMENTAL FIT

Choosing a college is very much like looking for a new home. The truth is that a college campus is going to be your home for a significant portion of the next two, four, or more years. Try to find a environment where you will feel comfortable as a citizen, a place that presents the social, cultural, and lifestyle comforts that you desire. Don't go looking for Utopia University or Perfect State College. Neither exists for many students. The important element here is to look for things you want and things you want to avoid. When you find the right balance in those elements, you probably have found colleges worthy of a closer look.

## AFFORDABILITY

The cost of college today cannot be dismissed as a factor in the selection process, but students and parents should attempt to separate, to the extent possible, financial issues from the academic and social factors. There was a time when the affordability issues were only a concern of the poor. Upward of two-thirds of the student body at many colleges are utilizing some form of financial aid.

Today, the financial concern casts a shadow across many families in many different economic categories. Before dismissing a college or university from consideration in the exploration process, the student should gather information about the availability of all forms of financial aid. When all financial aid options are considered, some institutions which first appear unaffordable, may, in fact, be more reasonably priced than others.

The U.S. Department of Education has created an interactive *College Scorecard*, which provides students and families with the critical information they need to make smart decisions about where to enroll for higher education, including a look at how cost may impact that decision. The Internet-based activity seeks to help students choose a school that is well-suited to meet their needs, priced affordably, and is consistent with their educational and career goals.

The *College Scorecard* provides students and families with a "snapshot" of clear information through an interactive tool that lets them choose among any number of options based on their individual needs—including location, size, campus setting, and degree and major programs. Each institutional *Scorecard* includes five key pieces of data about a college: costs, graduation rate, loan default rate, average amount borrowed, and employment. It is worth noting that critics of this Internet tool believe it overemphasizes the importance of cost and affordability in the college decision-making process. Readers can access the *College Scorecard* at: http://collegescorecard.ed.gov.

## ADMISSIBILITY

One of the things you will learn in your exploration of college options is how you "match up" with the requirements for admission and how closely you resemble the profile of the student the college wants to enroll. When you mirror the academic and personal characteristics of previously admitted and enrolled students, you are usually regarded as "admissible." One way to determine this is to examine the composite profile of the most recent first year class. How close do you resemble that group of students?

## READY, SET, GO

Your initial journey into college exploration can be an exciting time in your life . . . part of that "coming of age" that your parents, teachers, and other adults often talk about. Avoid the anxiety and discomfort that some students experience during this time by setting a course that is characterized by good planning and the use of all of the resources at your disposal.

If you have engaged in thorough examination of your abilities, aptitudes, goals, and interests, the chances are very likely that you will apply to colleges that will meet your needs, ones that will offer you the opportunity to continue to grow academically and socially. Ready, set, go!

## FREQUENTLY ASKED QUESTIONS

**Question:** Do you have any general advice to offer about managing the whole college admission process?
**Answer:** Two issues come to mind immediately. Give yourself sufficient time to do what needs to be done and remain organized throughout the experience. The time part will be explained in calendars that appear later in this guidebook and the presentation of tasks that you need to perform in a certain order. The organization part is, for some, more difficult. You are going to be collecting a lot of information and making a lot of notes and generating a lot of "stuff" during this process. Create a college-planning portfolio. A savvy

counselor once referenced the old adage, "A place for everything and everything in its place" when recommending the creation of a college-planning portfolio. You'd be wise to follow that guidance.

**Question:** As I examine prospective colleges, what should I be looking for?
**Answer:** Different students will apply different criteria to their examination. Your primary goal is to find the best possible place for you to learn. In addition, you want to study in an academic and social environment that is comfortable for you. Conduct a personal audit of all the things that are important to you and then apply those criteria to all the colleges and universities you encounter in your search.

That "different strokes for different folks" maxim certainly can be applied here. You might place a lot of importance on academic reputation of the college, availability of a major field of study, whether it has a lacrosse team, or how close it is to home. Your best friend, on the other hand, may be more interested in the success rate that graduates have in the work world, size, or type of community in which it is located.

Determine first the things that are important to you and then go about looking for colleges that have those characteristics. Remember, you're looking for the place where you are going to be learning and living for the next four or more years. Be thorough and you will most likely be successful.

**Question:** I've heard lots of "right" reasons for choosing a college. What are the wrong reasons?
**Answer:** There are many "wrong" reasons for selecting a college. The first that comes to mind is giving up control of the decision-making process and letting family or friends, even teachers and counselors, tell you the best place to go to college, and then doing exactly what they say. It's your life and your decision, and you need to keep control of both. Another common error is examining colleges based solely on cost. While cost is a very important element in the exploration and decision-making process, your primary concern should be with whether the college is the right place to both live and learn. If these conditions are not present, your chances of succeeding are at risk and the cost probably won't matter much.

**Question:** Is there a national database anywhere that will tell me the percentage of students that graduate from a particular college once they are admitted?
**Answer:** Yes, the graduation rate of students who enter a particular college is one of the features explorers will find on the *College Scorecard* created by the U.S. Department of Education. Go to: tp://www.whitehouse.gov/issues/education/higher-education/college-score-rd. After you enter the name of a

college, the graduation rate, along with other facts and figures, will be delivered electronically.

**Question:** What are the advantages of attending a community college?

**Answer:** Community college enrollment grew dramatically over the past half-decade because these institutions filled a vital education need of the nation. Many of the educational programs taught at the two-year level respond directly to the career objectives of their students. Second, community colleges allow developing students to continue their education (full- or part-time) and then transfer to a four-year college or university. Because community colleges are local and publicly supported, they also provide an affordable alternative for many students. Whether you are interested in obtaining a two-year associate's degree or just taking a refresher course in a particular subject, the community college is worthy of your full consideration.

**Question:** What are school-to-work programs?

**Answer:** The term "school--towork" is used to describe programs that help ease a high school student's transition from the classroom into the working world. Typically, students in these programs take courses part of the day and then work in a business that relates to their interests. The School-to-Work Opportunities Act, signed into law in 1994, funds efforts by parents, teachers, and business leaders to better prepare students for the world of work. Find out if there are school-to-work opportunities for you in your school or school district and then determine if one is right for you.

## STUDENT EXERCISE 2.1

### College Familiarity: Current and Future

1. In the spaces below list the colleges and universities with which you have some level of familiarity, but ones that you wish to examine in greater detail as you proceed through the exploration process:

   _____    _____
   _____    _____
   _____    _____
   _____    _____

2. In the spaces below list the colleges and universities with which you have little or no familiarity, ones that you will need to examine thoroughly as you proceed through the exploration process:

   _____    _____
   _____    _____
   _____    _____
   _____    _____

# Chapter 3

# A Calendar of Exploration, Decision-Making, and Application Tasks

In order to move progressively through the exploration, decision-making, and application process, the student needs to avoid the two Ps—pressure and procrastination. Pressure is typically self-inflicted when tasks are not completed according to required timetables. Such failure can have devastating results, especially when the task not completed on time is filing the application for admission or financial aid. The other enemy is procrastination—putting off until later what needs to be done now. Procrastination can lead to the pressure that many students feel throughout the process.

The Ps must be replaced with another one—planfulnning. A well-constructed and timely managed calendar of exploration, decision-making, and application tasks is the perfect antidote for pressure and procrastination. In addition to following a college readiness plan during the high school years, each explorer must become familiar with the calendar requirements and application nuances of the colleges and universities in which there is an interest. Once known, that information should be placed on a personal "to do" calendar and checked off as each task is completed.

Following is a year-by-year listing of some of the more significant tasks the explorer and applicant is likely to encounter:

## FIRST YEAR

Yes, the college-bound student must begin early in the high school experience to build an academic foundation and personal profile that colleges will look at favorably four years later.

1. Enroll in the courses that present the strongest academic challenge and allow you to make the most of the high school learning experience.
2. Begin to examine the educational and career goals that you may have already and create a plan that will lead you in that direction.
3. Recognize that interests and preferences will change as you get to know more about yourself, your achievements, and related factors, and be ready to adapt your goals based on these changes.
4. Register for and take any early high school tests that will identify your strengths, interests, and so on. Seek counselor's interpretation of this information when the findings come back to you.
5. Examine the extracurricular, service learning and other academic/non-academic activities available in the school and community. Venture into the ones that appeal to you.
6. Become an explorer of the world of work and use this early opportunity to learn more about specific careers.
7. Meet with your counselor to look at both long-and short-range goals and your initial progress toward achieving them.
8. Apply yourself in the classroom and in all the experiences you take on in pursuit of your education and career goals.

## SOPHOMORE YEAR

Success in the school-to-college transition may be measured in how well you address the responsibilities that are associated with becoming a good student, most notably the development of strong academic skills. Develop the ability to study and learn, and the result will be the kind of academic achievement that will enhance your future education options.

1. Meet with your counselor to review your program of studies in relation to the graduation requirements and the general requirements for admission to college. Conduct this audit within the context of a comprehensive high school plan and make certain that your current courses are reflective of where your abilities and interests suggest you should be in your sophomore year.
2. Talk with your teachers, counselor, and parents about your personal skills and competencies as a student. Identify your strengths and the areas that could be strengthened. See every opportunity to learn and practice study skills and habits such as note taking, time management, keyboard training, and reading efficiency.
3. Arrange to take a career aptitude test and/or interest inventory. These tools will identify possible fields for you to consider as you move

through high school and consider future educational and career options. Your counselor can suggest the appropriate tests and help you to interpret the findings.

4. Talk with your counselor and learn what you need to know about admission test use generally, as well as the specific test requirements of the institutions you are currently considering. Over the past several years the number of colleges to become test optional or to discontinue the use of admission test scores altogether has changed dramatically. Institutions requiring tests believe they play a role in identifying the students they want to educate. Others are attempting to discover new and different models for student selection.

5. Continue the process of self-awareness, the ongoing activity in which you analyze your aptitudes, achievements, interests, values, and goals.

6. Determine what tools (computerized guidance information systems) and resources (guides, viewbooks, DVDs) are available in your school's college and career resource center, guidance office, or library to assist you in exploring colleges. Start your exploration with the print information found in the general guides. Advance to the specific information that colleges offer prospective students at their Internet websites. Advance then to virtual tours and Internet exchanges (i.e. chat rooms, etc.) with colleges that offer such communication features. These resources, along with your counselor, teachers, and others, will become your information allies over the next couple of years.

7. Learn how to use the informational tools and resources of the school and community library. See if any college libraries in your community can offer you similar exposure.

8. Set aside some time in your personal schedule to engage in leisure reading, practice your computer keyboard skills, or participate in sports and activities away from the classroom. Learn what you can from monitoring college social media sites. Most colleges want to admit the "well-rounded" person, but some students can go overboard. Become engaged in one or two extracurricular activities rather than spread thinly across many.

9. Start a list of the things that will be important to you in the selection of a college and think about the questions you will need to ask in order to gather this information.

10. Study hard and maximize every learning opportunity available to you. You'll thank yourself in a couple of years.

A solid sophomore year experience will add to the foundation you have started and will serve you well through the rest of the high school experience.

Moreover, the habits and skills you acqui early on will serve you through high school, college, and on into the caree world.

## JUNIOR YEAR

You've reached or have passed the middl of your high school experience. While college may seem like it is way ( in the future somewhere, your junior year is the time to give more struct e to your exploration so that you fully match your educational achievemen , aptitudes, and interests with all viable options. Consider the following act ities:

1. Continue to apply yourself in the cl; room. Junior courses, especially those in a college preparatory curricu m, are more intensive and teachers are likely to be expecting more o you. However, the academic and personal skills that you are now lear ng to master will serve you for a lifetime, and are essential for succes n college.

2. Meet again with your counselor to r iew your academic schedule and the progress you're making. As you egin to create the list of colleges that interest you, compare your a demic profile with the specific admission requirements at those inst tions. Remember that admission officers see many applications from ospective students that meet their requirements. Therefore, your best c nces for admission will be if you meet and surpass the basic requirem ts.

3. Schedule and take the ACT, SAT, or ny related standardized tests that you and your counselor determine ay be required for admission to college, remembering that a larger nu ber adhere "test optional" policy today (See National Center for Fai and Open Testing list at https://www.fairtest.org). Determine any te, format, (print or digital), or other options. Participate in any test rep classes that may be available through your school or community ganizations or available via fee-charging commercial services. Revi w the results of any preliminary tests that you have taken and schedu the next round of tests. Consult with your teachers and counselor al ut how you might improve your test scores. Continue to take subje tests and Advanced Placement exams as you complete the appropri e courses.

4. Mount a serious information-gatheri g campaign, one that allows you to match prospective colleges to you personal abilities, achievements, interests, and learning objectives. C neral college guides and institutional viewbooks are an excellent w y to initiate your research. Then step up to the more specific inforn tion that colleges present about admission and financial aid on spe fic websites. Take advantage of

computerized guidance information programs and college videotapes in the guidance department or library. Attend college fairs (small, medium and large variations) and special seminars offered by admission offices to disseminate information about the admission and financial aid processes and assist in completing applications.

5. Learn as much as you can about financial aid, beginning with the definitions of such terms as merit-based aid, need-based aid, scholarships, and loans. As you study colleges see what financial aid is directed at the students they admit and become familiar with the requirements for this assistance. In addition, take a look at national and local scholarships and determine your eligibility for winning this type of award.

6. Arrange a personal meeting with your counselor to get the individual attention that you might need to gather information and consider educational options after high school. Your counselor can direct you to appropriate resources and then assist in the evaluation and use of the information you have acquired.

7. If you haven't already, start the process of visiting the colleges that are at the top of your interest list. Arrange to tour the campus, sit in on a class, attend a concert or athletic event, and meet with admission counselors to get the answers to your specific questions and learn more about each institution. Make every attempt to visit colleges when they are in session. Stay in a dorm if permissible. Look around the city or community in which the college is located. Continue your campus visits into the summer and on into the fall of your senior year.

8. Organize all of the information you are collecting about colleges (e.g., applications, admission and financial aid resources, multimedia sources, college fair notes and other items) into a college planning portfolio. As the volume of information grows greater, a portfolio will help you organize and manage this information.

9. Interact regularly with your parents to keep them informed about where your exploration is taking you and allow them to track your progress and define ways in which they can be supportive. Encourage them to read the guides and viewbooks, take the virtual tours, accompany you to college fairs and campus visits, and participate in counseling programs designed for parents.

10. Begin the process of refining your list and learn as much as you can about these colleges. It will soon be time to identify a final list of colleges where you will file applications.

11. Consider using the summer between your junior and senior year to enroll in a class at a local college or to participate in a special seminar (e.g., creative writing, keyboard training). Otherwise, work at a summer job, relax, and prepare for that final year.

Can you believe it? Only your senior ye[ar] stands between you and the college experience. You continue to evolve a[nd] grow as an individual as do the expectations that your parents, teachers, a[nd] others have of you. Get ready! Your senior year lies just ahead.

## SENIOR YEAR

You're in the countdown year—the final year of high school. In just a short time you will be making final decisions and applying for admission to college. It will be a very exciting and busy year, a time for you to address the following tasks:

1. Refine or reduce the list of colleges you have under consideration to a manageable number. For most, it will be a number up to three—for others three to five—and for some, five or more. There is no magic number! The final list should encompass a combination of "safety," "probable," and "reach" colleges.
2. Keep colleges on the list that you are really interested in attending. Locate the admission and financial aid forms (print or electronic) for your narrowing list on the various college websites. Determine if your choices will accept the Common Application. Most colleges will give you the option of completing and submitting these forms online. Others will let you complete the forms online which you can print and send via regular mail. Elect whatever admission application submission action is most comfortable for you.
3. Meet once again with your counselor to review your academic record and current courses in light of the list of schools where you want to file applications. Arrange to have a current (and eventually final) transcript of your grades forwarded to these colleges where this official school document will become a part of your admission application. Review the tasks you need to complete as you move through your senior year and get answers to questions that remain.
4. Determine what admission, achievement, and related tests you may need to take during the coming months and register accordingly. Determine and select from any test dates and formats (print or digital) that may be available. Consult with your counselor regarding the benefits of repeating one or more of these examinations. If you are seeking collegiate credit for Advanced Placement courses, then be sure to register and complete the appropriate AP tests.
5. As you begin to review the admission applications and financial aid forms, create a checklist and calendar for each important milestone and

deadline. Note that applications for early decision and early action must be filed much earlier. Review and update your checklist on a regular basis. Earlier in this guidebook the suggestion of creating a college planning portfolio was offered. As you narrow your list of colleges where you intend to make application, having a "file within a file" for each application makes a great deal of sense.

6. If you will be applying for any type of financial aid, you will need to acquire and complete the Free Application for Federal Student Aid (FAFSA). Some colleges will require that you submit the CSS/Profile and/or their institutional aid application. Your counselor will have copies or you can find them on the Internet. Check deadlines for state aid programs and file forms accordingly.

7. Conduct your campus visits (live or virtual) or participate in any remaining college fairs that will provide answers to questions that remain before you embark on the application process.

8. Set aside some time for the orderly completion of college applications and related forms. Pass along any teacher and counselor recommendations that must be completed in support of your application. This process should begin in mid-to late October. Note that some colleges will request an essay or writing sample. Address this task early so that it receives the appropriate attention. If you are applying for private scholarships or participating in academic competitions, be aware of their requirements and deadlines.

9. Continue to communicate with your counselor. Your school will be required to send an official transcript of your academic record and related information to the college(s). Once you are certain that you are going to make application, forward the appropriate forms and directions to your counselor.

10. Continue to devote the required attention to your senior classes. Your acceptance at any college will be conditional upon the satisfactory completion of your senior classes. Don't slack off!

11. If you have applied to more than one college, rank your preferences so that you can address multiple acceptances when colleges inform you of their admission decision. Your decision can be complicated by placement on the wait-list at a particular college. If you are not accepted at any of the college(s) where you have applied, another visit to your counselor will allow you to review your options.

12. Once you have made your final decision about where to enroll, send your deposit, housing forms, and related materials. Review the student orientation packets and college course selection forms as they are received. Say "thank you" to everyone that helped you.

Finally, take a bit of time to consider what you have accomplished and be proud that you are about to enter a new phase of your life . . . the world of a college student.

## FREQUENTLY ASKED QUESTIONS

**Question:** Even if I maintain an orderly schedule for gathering information and completing the tasks associated with the various calendars, how will I know that I am on track?

**Answer:** At the beginning of the college exploration process, you "don't know what you don't know." With each step of the exploration and decision-making process, additional information will be revealed. Many of your questions will be answered just by the exploration process itself. Information can also generate new questions. Your sophomore inquiry will be somewhat general, followed by a more learned and targeted inquiry in your junior year. The senior and application year is far more focused. et behind and you lose valuable control. Remember the most important P word—planning.

## STUDENT EXERCISE 3.1

### Things to Do Calendar

Review the tasks in the sections that preceded this exercise and make a personal list of "things to do" as you proceed through the exploration, decision-making, and application processes. Note each task on the calendar and check it or cross it off when completed.

First-Year Tasks                  Completed

_____

_____

_____

_____

Sophomore-Year Tasks          Completed

_____

_____

_____

_____

Junior-Year Tasks                Complete

_____

_____

_____

_____

Senior-Year Tasks                Complete

_____

_____

_____

_____

*Chapter 4*

# The First Step

*Taking a Look at You*

As you embark on your study of educational options, it is important to begin by taking a long, deliberate look at yourself. Who are you? What are your likes and dislikes? What do you consider your academic strengths and weaknesses? Do you know what you want to study? Have you determined the career or careers that interest you? What are you looking for in the type, size, or location of a college? And maybe the most important question—why are you going to college?

That's a daunting list of questions and you may have others to add to the list. Your personalized set of exploratory questions will become the framework of a self-awareness study. No matter how much you may think you know about college and its place in your future, it's important to first step back and examine yourself. This self-examination may validate or affirm things you already know, but more importantly, it may shed light on something that you don't know and need to know in order to move successfully through the remainder of your high school experience and on to college.

By gaining a full understanding of yourself, you can personalize the entire college exploration and selection process. When it comes time to make decisions, you'll be making them in full consideration of the person that will be called upon to implement them—you!

During your youth, you have no doubt become aware of the individual characteristics that you possess that are similar to and different from your peers. These characteristics include aptitudes, achievements, interests, personality traits, values, lifestyle preferences, and goals: elements that will impact your educational and career development. They are the things that contribute to your individuality.

Awareness of these characteristics will allow you to make decisions that are consistent with that individuality. Failure to conduct periodic audits of these traits is an error that can have significant consequences on your future success.

*Aptitudes* represent your capacity for learning, your natural ability to do something. When someone makes the statement, "He's/she's a natural," when referring to one's ability in music, athletics, or some other area of endeavor, they are really speaking of his or her exceptional aptitude in these areas. Others may have an aptitude or unusual capacity for learning in science, mathematics, writing, or other studies.

*Achievements* are the measured accomplishments in your life, those things that you have done well. In school, progress is measured regularly and reported to you in the form of grades or academic awards. In athletics, performances are measured by a stopwatch or statistics. In music, art, or theater, your achievements may result in recognition or praise for a job well done. It is possible to achieve or become accomplished in something for which you have little or limited aptitude. This is usually the result of concentration and hard work.

*Interests* are the things you like to do, commanding your time and arousing your curiosity. Sometimes, interests are spin-offs of your aptitudes and achievements as they represent areas where you have devoted study and attention and earned some degree of success. Other interests are outlets or diversions, things you do simply for fun.

*Personality traits* are those characteristics that make one person different from another. In psychology, personality is defined as the total physical, intellectual, and emotional structure of a person, including his or her aptitudes, abilities, and interests. Words like outgoing, quiet, inquisitive, and intellectual are often used to describe people. Knowing your own personality traits can help you define educational and career environments that are conducive to the person that you are.

*Values* are the aspects of your life that you hold in esteem, things you would prefer if you had a choice. Any examination of self-awareness would be incomplete without some analysis of the values you possess and how they relate to your development. For example, prestige and status may be important to you, but mean less to a classmate.

As all of these characteristics emerge in young adulthood, *lifestyle preferences* take shape. These are the ways you prefer to spend your time. Many prefer the "hustle and bustle" of city life while others prefer the calm and slow pace offered by small communities or rural areas. Some will become passionate about their careers and throw themselves into their work, often spending hours upon hours in their career pursuits. Others will prefer to escape regularly and pursue non-career things away from work. As you grow older these preferences become even more pronounced and play a major role in your behavior and the goals you set for the future.

Many personal characteristics are apparent and straightforward and seem to be well rooted and ever present. Others are evolving and more difficult to recognize. Stop from time to time and revisit these characteristics. You'll be glad you did!

Once you have conducted a thorough examination of your personal characteristics and traits, it's time to tie that information to a goal or goals. Why are you going to college? Recent studies have revealed a pragmatic answer as students say they would like to achieve economic security and career success. A recent edition of the UCLA Higher Education Research Institute (HERI) American College Freshman study reported that students considered their own learning and future career opportunities important reasons for going to college. Specifically, that report ranked the four following reasons as most important: 1) Learn more about things that interest me (87%), 2) To be able to get a better job (82%), 3) To gain a general education and appreciation of ideas (80%) and 4) To get training for a specific career (76%).

Students have a greater chance of succeeding in their educational pursuits if they find a learning and living environment that is compatible with and supportive of their aptitudes, achievements, interests, personality traits, values, and lifestyle preferences, one that will assist them in realizing their educational goals.

## FREQUENTLY ASKED QUESTIONS

**Question:** I'm trying to decide if I really want to go to college. Will a degree make a difference in my future earning power?
**Answer:** Studies conducted by the U.S. Census Bureau give meaning to the theory that "the more you learn—the more you earn." Following are recent median annual income levels by educational attainment: less than high school—$31,326, high school diploma—$48,708, some college (no degree)—$61,911, associate's degree—$69,573, bachelor's degree—$100,164, master's degree—$117,439, doctorate—$142,347, and professional (doctorate in medicine, law, etc.) degree—$162,127. Another important thing to note: Unemployment rates go down for persons as their educational attainment rates go up. While this fact is generally accurate, a Georgetown Center of Education and Work study has found that in some occupational clusters and fields, the dichotomy is not that dramatic.

**Question:** I've read that a lot of high profile and successful people dropped out of or didn't go to college? Is this accurate?

**Answer:** Start with Bill Gates at Microsoft, Mark Zuckerberg at Facebook and the late Steve Jobs at Apple Computer and you have three fairly recent examples of very successful individuals who dropped out of college.

Television pioneer Ted Turner of CNN and TBS cable networks followed a different path to non-graduation. He was expelled from college—on two occasions.

If you want to go back in history, President Abraham Lincoln had little formal education. He taught himself trigonometry to order to become a surveyor and read law books in order to pass the bar and become an attorney.

Except for the traditional occupations like teacher, lawyer and engineer, many people have been known to access their chosen careers via non-traditional routes. Many entrepreneurs in the world of business, for example, built their companies and businesses from the ground up by rolling up their sleeves and jumping head first into their work. While college studies resulting in degree attainment can never be overvalued, other routes to success remain a possibility for many.

**Question:** How true is it that the most successful people are the ones that attended elite colleges?

**Answer:** Harvard, Stanford, Duke, the University of California at Berkeley and other colleges with elite reputations have produced more than their fair share of successful women and men of business, government, military, entertainment and other fields, but these institutions are by no means the only path to success in the workplace. President Lyndon Johnson (Texas State Teachers College, now Texas State University—San Marcus), television hostess, actress and businesswoman Oprah Winfrey (Tennessee State University), billionaire businessman Warren Buffet (University of Nebraska at Lincoln), and Secretary of State and U.S. Army General Colin Powell (City College of New York) are just a few examples.

**Question:** If I haven't made a final career decision, how can I choose a college that's right for me?

**Answer:** Relax. Your final career decision can follow your college decision. If you have some idea of what you want to do (e.g., engineering, business, communications), you can use your college studies to validate that interest. You may need to consider colleges that allow you the flexibility to continue your exploration. If you have absolutely no idea as to your future career, look for a college where you can use the first couple of years to get some of the basic degree requirements completed while you continue the process of career exploration and discovery. Remember, too, the value associated with learning to learn. There is a lot to be said for studying for the enrichment of life and allowing your career ambitions to fall into place later.

If you want to engage in more intensive career exploration at this time, talk to your counselor about taking a career interest inventory and consider getting some hands-on experiences in the work world to see if any occupation or career field begins to appeal to you. You might participate in any "college and career readiness" programs that are being created at both the secondary and postsecondary education levels.

**Question:** Is it bad to list my major as "undecided" on my application if asked? **Answer:** In a perfect world, every college applicant would know what he or she wanted to study in college and do in a future career. But we all know how imperfect this world happens to be. You may still be in the process of discovering your abilities, aptitudes, and interests and linking these characteristics with future career and lifestyle preferences. For many, this will continue throughout your young adult years. It is perfectly acceptable to indicate "undecided" on your application. In fact, undecided is one of the more popular majors of incoming freshmen at many colleges.

## STUDENT EXEl CISE 4.1

**Personal Characteristics Audit: Takin  a Look at You**

Complete the answers to the following qu  tions. Review your answers peri-
odically and update any information that   )es not reflect your current view
of your personal characteristics.

1. Make a list of five adjectives you fe  your friends/fellow students and
   teachers/counselor would use to des  be you:
   Friends/fellow students:
   1. _____
   2. _____
   3. _____
   4. _____
   5. _____
   Teachers/counselor:
   1. _____
   2. _____
   3. _____
   4. _____
   5. _____

2. Make a list of five adjectives you w  ld use to describe yourself:
   1. _____
   2. _____
   3. _____
   4. _____
   5. _____

3. What do you consider to be you  greatest personal strengths or
   attributes?

   _____      _____
   _____      _____
   _____      _____
   _____      _____

4. What do you consider to be your gre  est weaknesses or shortcomings?

   _____      _____
   _____      _____
   _____      _____
   _____      _____

5. List three academic subjects or interests you would like to continue to study:
   1. _____
   2. _____
   3. _____

6. Which high school courses have you enjoyed the most?

   _____
   _____
   _____
   _____

7. Which high school courses have presented the biggest challenges or
   posed the most difficulty?

   _____
   _____
   _____
   _____

8. Identify a recent experience (school or non-school) that stimulated your
   intellectual curiosity:

   _____
   _____
   _____
   _____

9. How would you describe your academic performance to date? Is your
   high school record a true reflection of your academic ability and potential? If not, how would you characterize your ability and potential to
   succeed in college?

   _____
   _____
   _____
   _____

## STUDENT EXE  CISE 4.2

**Setting Personal Educational and Ca  er Goals**

1. What is your immediate educational  al? Why are you going to college
   or on to postsecondary education?

   _____         _____
   _____         _____
   _____         _____
   _____         _____

2. What would you like to study? Have  ou decided on a college major or
   specific program of study?

   _____         _____
   _____         _____
   _____         _____
   _____         _____

3. What is your eventual educational   al (e.g., bachelor's degree, master's, etc.)?

   _____         _____
   _____         _____
   _____         _____
   _____         _____

4. Have you set a career goal or identi  d a field (e.g., business, communication, health, public service, etc.)  1 which you would like to work?
   If yes, what is that occupation or fie  ?

   _____         _____
   _____         _____
   _____         _____
   _____         _____

5. To what extent is your college choic  relevant to your career goals?

   _____         _____
   _____         _____
   _____         _____
   _____         _____

6. What do you consider to be your strongest academic (e.g., writing, computation, analytical) skills? To what extent do you wish to pursue collegiate studies related to these skills?

_____

_____

_____

_____

*Chapter 5*

# Mounting a Search

## *Getting Answers to Your College Questions*

During the exploration process the student will have an opportunity to ask a lot of questions in order to find the colleges that meet the academic, environmental, and financial requirements that he or she has established as important. The decision whether to apply to a college will be tied directly to the information that is collected and the impressions that are made during this evaluative process. This chapter will offer information about the various forms of postsecondary education and present a host of questions that explorers may want to include in their search.

## TYPES OF INSTITUTIONS

Here at the beginning of the search process, let's take just a minute to review the various forms of postsecondary education available to students. When you consider the full array of educational opportunities, you'll understand why it is so important to do a good job of exploring.

When you finish high school, you can continue your education at a four-year college or university, a two-year community, junior or technical college or at a specialized career or vocational institute. Later on, you may wish to pursue additional study at a graduate or professional school.

## DEGREE GRANTING COLLEGES AND UNIVERSITIES

The National Center for Education Statistics has identified nearly 4,000 degree granting postsecondary institutions (four- and two-year) in the

United States, a number which is always in flux due to openings, closings, and mergers.

- These institutions typically prepare graduates in targeted studies (e.g., engineering, business, education, information sciences, etc.) or the more general study of liberal arts.
- A majority of four-year institutions are privately or publicly supported and more likely to offer a campus living and housing environment.
- Admission to four-year institutions is generally competitive, meaning students must meet specific institution defined requirements for entry.
- Admission to two-year (community, junior and technical colleges) is often open, but some study areas may be competitive.
- A bachelor's or baccalaureate degree is awarded to students completing four years of study
- An associate degree and certificates are awarded to students completing two years of study or completion of defined body of knowledge and/or mastery of a particular skillset.
- A growing number of institutions, many that are proprietary or for-profit in structure, are moving into the world of distance learning and offering students the opportunity to earn a degree via the Internet.
- Both four-and two-year institutions are accredited by professional and regional accreditation bodies.

## CAREER, TECHNICAL OR VOCATIONAL INSTITUTE

- The Accrediting Commission of Career Schools and Colleges (ACCSC) lists 700 accredited career, technical and vocational institutions.
- A greater percentage of these institutions are proprietary or for-profit in structure.
- Training is focused and varies in duration, from a few weeks to a year or more in length.
- Completion of a course of study often results in the awarding of a certificate by the institution or the preparation for a government issued license or certificate (i.e., practical nursing, child care attendant, etc.).
- Admission is open. Some study area will set enrollment or admission requirements.
- Study is often characterized by a "hands on" or "learn by doing" approach and may entail an internship or field experience as a requirement.
- Diplomas and/or certificates are awarded to students who complete programs.

## INSTITUTIONAL CHARACTERISTICS

Following are a number of questions that you, the student, should ask as part of this exploration. The list should not be viewed as exhaustive (you will certainly think of others), and they are not presented in any kind of priority order.

## PROGRAM OF STUDY, ACADEMIC PHILOSOPHY, REPUTATION

Does the college offer the academic specialty you wish to pursue? What is the academic reputation of the institution in general and the program (e.g., journalism, engineering) in particular? Do graduates get good jobs and are they admitted to grad school? Does the college have a strong library and use the latest tools and technology to educate its students? What are the requirements for success in the classroom? Does the institution ascribe to a particular philosophy of teaching or learning? What is the typical class size? Do the best professors teach classes at the undergraduate level?

## ADMISSION REQUIREMENTS AND COMPETITION

How will your abilities, aptitudes, interests and previous achievements stack up against other applicants and enrolled students? How have students with your academic credentials fared in the admission process? What is the profile of the typical student at the college? What percentage of admitted students graduate? In how many years?

## LOCATION, SETTING, AND SIZE

Are you interested in going to a college nearby, in the state or region, or anywhere in the United States or the world? Do you have a preference for the type of community (e.g., large city, small city, rural) where the college is located? How important is the campus setting (e.g., open spaces and tree-filled lawns versus high-rise buildings)? How close or far from home would you like to be? Do you have a preference as to enrollment size?

## INSTITUTIONAL CHARACTERISTICS

What type of institution best suits your academic and environmental needs? Do you prefer a large university with multiple academic venues, a small liberal arts college, or something in between? Do you want to study at a two-year or four-year college? Do you prefer a public or private, coeducational or single-sex, church-affiliated, or career-oriented institution? Would you consider an online or distance learning experience?

## ACCOMMODATIONS

Are the dormitories comfortable and well furnished? Will the food service respond to your dietary needs? Can your physical fitness and recreational interests be satisfied? Is living on campus mandatory? What percentage of students live off campus?

## SOCIAL, CULTURAL, EXTRACURRICULAR ATMOSPHERE

What social, cultural, and leisure time opportunities are available? Do you have interests outside of the classroom (e.g., music, sports, drama, volunteer work) that you would like to maintain while in college? If so, will the college or the community allow you to pursue those interests? Is there a church, synagogue, mosque, or other related congregation on campus or in the community that will satisfy your faith-based interests?

## SPECIAL NEEDS OR CONSIDERATIONS

Can the college respond to tutorial, counseling, health, or other special needs that you might have? Does the campus and surrounding community present a secure living environment? If you have any type of disability, can the college accommodate any special needs that require attention?

## COST

What is the cost of tuition, room and board, and other fees? What personal (e.g., transportation) costs will be required? What financial aid opportunities exist, and what are the qualifications? Is financial need factored into the admission decision? Are there opportunities for part-time work on campus or in the community?

## STUDENTS WITH SPECIAL CONCERNS

A considerable number of college-bound students fall into one or more groups with special concerns. In addition to asking all of the general questions presented in this guidebook, these applicants to college must get answers to questions that are pertinent to their special needs. These students include the following:

## ADULT LEARNERS AND NON-TRADITIONAL STUDENTS

Adult learners (sometimes referred to as non-traditional students) represent individuals of all ages that have found their way to or back to college. They may be first-timers or "zoomers," students who found their college experience interrupted for some reason and are attempting to "resume" their studies and earn a degree.

Many adult students are veterans of military service who elected to serve their country and are now using their college benefits to help defray the costs of college. Others are on part-time or flexible schedules attempting to balance work and study in the hopes of earning a degree. Finally, adult learners can be seniors who are studying for self-enhancement or recreational purposes.

Many colleges have found that the life experiences and maturity of adult learners add to the general diversity of their academic and social environment and encourage their enrollment. Some have created services to assist those away from education for a time to become reoriented as students and get back in the academic groove.

Along with the general questions (e.g., programs of study, size, location, etc.), adult learners may wish to inquire about the atmosphere that will exist for them as non-traditional learners and what services they can expect to find on the campus once enrolled.

## HOMESCHOOLED STUDENTS

A recent report conducted by the National Home Education Research Institute stated that there were about 3.7 million homeschooled students in 2020–2021 in grades K-12 in the United States (roughly 6% to 7% of school-age children), a statistic that exploded upward due to the coronavirus pandemic and is expected to stay higher for some time. These homeschooled students, like their college-bound peers in traditional school environments, must get answers to the same academic, person-social, and related questions.

College-bound homeschoolers will not have or may be limited in their access to the formal assistance offered by school counselors. This means they must rely more heavily on the guidance of their parents, family, friends and the assistance of college admission and financial aid professionals when they are exploring and making decisions.

Although homeschoolers take a different academic and social route to high school completion, their path to admission is likely to be the same as their traditionally educated counterparts. They must complete the same forms, take the same admission tests and complete all of the tasks that every applicant must execute. They must also study and learn the intricacies of college (e.g., formal schedules, large lectures, etc.), as well as living in a diverse environment. These things will be considerably different from homeschooling and future enrollees need to be prepared to make the appropriate adjustments.

Most of the barriers and misconceptions that once suppressed opportunities for homeschooled students have been eliminated or drastically reduced. Colleges, for the most part, recognize the quality of the academic preparation of homeschoolers and welcome their applications for admission. All that remains is for homeschooled students to engage in a thorough examination of their personal goals and college preferences, followed by a thorough examination of the institutions that can meet those needs and expectations.

## INTERNATIONAL STUDENTS

American colleges and universities are very popular with students from around the globe, a factor that is likely to grow with time. Applicants from outside the United States will find strong competition for enrollment. Applicants should begin early and engage in careful exploration if they are to be successful in achieving admission. While many colleges have expanded their international recruitment efforts, especially for those students who are "full-pay," some of the admission criteria and protocols bear study.

International students who will need financial assistance, for example, should not waste energy and time applying to institutions that do not award financial assistance to international students.

Since your academic and personal credentials will be examined and evaluated differently by different colleges, applicants must determine exactly what is expected of them in the admission process. Unlike many countries that have a universal admission system for all students, U.S. colleges operate independently and each has its own admission criteria and procedures.

Applicants from around the world must convince each American college of how they will positively affect the academic, cultural, and social aspects of college life. That persuasion, to the extent possible, should be conveyed via the application, interview and essay. If English is not the native language of the applicant or one that she or he has mastered, it will be measured by taking the Test of English as a Foreign Language (TOEFL) in addition to any required ACT, SAT and SAT Subject Tests.

Generally, a citizen of a foreign country who wishes to enter the United States must first obtain a visa, either a non-immigrant visa for a temporary stay, or an immigrant visa for permanent residence. You must have a student visa to study in the United States. Your course of study and the type of school you plan to attend determine whether you need an F-1 visa or an M-1 visa. The U.S. State Department has posted information about visa acquisition at https://travel.state.gov/content/travel/en/us-visas/study.html.

Students should seek the assistance of counselors, former international students who have studied in the United States, and, the college admission officers designated to work with international students. Each will shed light on the admission and financial process and contribute to a realistic application and smooth enrollment process. International applicants will find the following website of US News & World Report useful in learning which colleges enroll the greatest numbers of international students: http://colleges.usnews. rankingsandreviews.com/best-colleges/rankings/national-universities/ most-international.

## STUDENTS WITH DISABILITIES

In the past students with disabilities, both learning and physical, have not participated in the college experience at the same levels as other students. That, however, has changed and more students with disabilities are finding ways to meet the challenges of college study and living. At the same time institutions create programs and services designed to accommodate special learning or physical needs.

Students with disabilities are not required to disclose their disability at any time and a college is prohibited by federal law from asking about a disability on the application form. Students who believe a disability has had a negative impact on their grades or test scores should take time to explain their personal situation to an admission counselor. Students with a physical disability need to determine how "disability friendly" prospective campuses will be and factor that criterion into their exploration and decision making.

Each college has a responsibility under federal law to ensure access to all educational programs and activities by students with disabilities. Each has established an office of disabled student services that will use educational and medical documentation in providing programs, services, and related accommodations that bring about that access.

The Association on Higher Education and Disability (AHEAD) provides student, parent, and transition information through a series of Frequently Asked Questions (FAQs) on the organization's website located at http://www.ahead.org/students-parents.

## TRANSFER STUDENTS

A large and growing number of students earn their degree at a college different from the one where they originally enrolled. Studies conducted by the National Association for College Admission Counseling (NACAC) reveal that one in three students will likely transfer to other colleges, a number that includes community college students completing two-year degrees and transferring to a four-year degree program.

Students transfer for numerous reasons (academic, personal, financial, etc.), but they must engage in the same exploration strategies they used in selecting their original college and possibly do even a better job at it than they did the first time. Transferring can be very competitive as the targeted college will use the student's grades in their current college in making its admission decision. Another reason for the increased competition is the limited number of upper-class openings that are available any given academic year.

Often colleges are open about what they expect from transfer students and that should be addressed directly and honestly. A review of admission criteria, first year class profile, and transfer guidelines are essential ingredients in the transfer process. Current college students will also be interested in knowing how many of their credits are transferable you don't want to repeat courses or lose credit by transferring. The student interested in transferring should examine a college that has a "transfer-friendly" reputation and be open and positive about their reasons for transferring.

Finally, students who have transferred and admission officers who specialize in working with transfer students can be important allies in helping prospective transfer students understand the complexities of the process and how to make it happen.

## IMPORTANT QUESTIONS REQUIRE ANSWERS

The uniqueness of personal needs and circumstances should not be a deterrent to the exploration and decision-making process. Addressing such concerns may take a little more time to complete, but the rewards will be well worth the investment.

Few colleges will earn a five-star rating in each of these areas of exploration. In the final analysis, does the college present you with a good feeling? Is it a place where you see yourself learning and living over the next four or more years? If the answer is "yes," the next step is to get an application for admission.

## RECENT GLOBAL EVENTS ALTER INSTITUTIONS AND THE WAY THEY EDUCATE

The global coronavirus pandemic that first occurred in 2020 had a tremendous effect on every aspect of American education. From full to partial closings to a major expansion of remote education systems and other changes in procedures and protocols, postsecondary education institutions had to develop a "new normal" in order to continue their services to students. Even the best of these modifications wasn't enough to disturb student habits and behaviors and lead to even harsher consequences for many. As a result, student enrollment dropped significantly in some places and students

## FREQUENTLY ASKED QUESTIONS

**Question:** How can I determine the particular reputation of a school or department within a college that I'm considering?
**Answer:** You've hit upon one of the problems associated with "rating" and "ranking" guides. Often there are exemplary departments within less than exemplary institutions. These may be overlooked if the student goes only by the general reputation of the college or university. Sometimes national professional associations accredit study programs, and career entry may be limited if you fail to get your degree from an accredited institution. Ask someone currently in the profession if such an accreditation program exists.

Otherwise, the best barometer may be the impressions of recent graduates or those students currently enrolled in the program of study. The answer to a question as simple as "do graduates find employment in their career field" or "do graduates gain admission to gradua  school" can tell you a great deal about the reputation of the department or  hool.

**Question:** How great is the risk of unem  oyment after college if I elect to study the wrong thing?

**Answer:** First, you need to know unem  yment is greater for those who have earned a high school diploma and e  n worse for those who dropped out. College graduates will find that son  fields of study are riskier than others, due to the numbers of people prep  ing for or already in the employment pipeline.

The Georgetown Center for Education  d the Workforce has been tracking unemployment by college majors. Th  study found that degree holders will generally fare better in finding em  oyment than non-grads, not all degrees are created equal, and applicants  o college may wish to do more career exploration than previously thought  ecessary to avoid unemployment.

A number of factors influence the jol  narket. The recent construction and housing decline, for example, has  affected architecture graduates. Unemployment is generally higher for  ion-technical majors, including graduates of the arts and social sciences.  echnology and information science graduates find more opportunities tl  n many, as do degree holders in education, healthcare, and the STEM (Sci  ce, Technology, Engineering and Mathematics) studies.

Job openings occur for two reasons—tl  growth and expansion of a field or the exodus or retirement of large nun  ers of people. Students, before and after enrolling in college, should kec  an eye on the trends presented regularly by the *Occupational Outlook Ho  lbook* and *Occupational Outlook Quarterly* (both available online and in pri  editions) of the U.S. Department of Labor Bureau of Labor Statistics.

**Question:** Will I be taught by professor  or teaching assistants? How can I find out?

**Answer:** You've probably heard that the  est professors at some colleges are only teaching graduate classes or are  levoting their academic time to research, writing, and related scholarly  ork. Unfortunately for you, this may be the case. In response to the increas  g number of times they are being asked this question, many colleges are ma  ng available information regarding the number and/or percentage of unde  raduate classes that are taught by professors versus those taught by teaching  ssistants. You can ask the admission office for this information.

## STUDENT EXERCISE 5.1

### College and University Characteristics:
### Exploring Your Personal Preferences

Listed below are the characteristics most students look for when selecting a college. Review the entire list of criteria and then go back and evaluate each according to its importance. Very Important means the characteristic will weigh heavily in your future evaluation of the college. Somewhat Important suggests the presence of this characteristic would enhance your future consideration of the college. Not Important means the characteristic will have no bearing on or does not apply to your consideration of colleges at this time.

These characteristics should not be viewed as an exhaustive list. You may have other or more specific items that you would like to see present in the colleges that you are considering. Use the blank spaces found at various points on the profile to insert these personal exploration characteristics.

| Exploration Criteria | Very Important | Somewhat Important | Not Important |
|---|---|---|---|
| 1. Academic Reputation | _____ | _____ | _____ |
|    a. General reputation of the college | _____ | _____ | _____ |
|    b. Specific reputation of the major or program of study | _____ | _____ | _____ |
| 2. Curriculum or Program of Study | _____ | _____ | _____ |
|    a. Availability of the major or specific program I want to study | _____ | _____ | _____ |
|    b. Availability of first-rate general or liberal arts curriculum | _____ | _____ | _____ |
| 3. Academic Support Services | _____ | _____ | _____ |
|    a. Availability of special services (e.g., tutoring, advising, etc.). List requirements below: | _____ | _____ | _____ |
|    b. _____ | _____ | _____ | _____ |
|    c. _____ | _____ | _____ | _____ |
|    d. _____ | _____ | _____ | _____ |

| Exploration Criteria | Very Important | Somewhat Important | Not Important |
|---|---|---|---|
| 4. Academic Philosophy and Instructional Style | ____ | ____ | ____ |
|    a. Class size | ____ | ____ | ____ |
|    b. Undergraduate access to experienced professors and teachers | ____ | ____ | ____ |
|    c. _____ | ____ | ____ | ____ |
| 5. Type or Affiliation of Institution | ____ | ____ | ____ |
|    a. Public | ____ | ____ | ____ |
|    b. Private | ____ | ____ | ____ |
|    c. Special focus (e.g., career training) | ____ | ____ | ____ |
|    d. Two year | ____ | ____ | ____ |
|    e. Four year | ____ | ____ | ____ |
|    f. Single sex | ____ | ____ | ____ |
|    g. Coeducational | ____ | ____ | ____ |
|    h. Historically black college/ university | ____ | ____ | ____ |
|    i. Religious affiliation | ____ | ____ | ____ |
|    j. Military affiliation | ____ | ____ | ____ |
|    k. _____ | ____ | ____ | ____ |
|    l. _____ | ____ | ____ | ____ |
| 6. Academic Facilities and Student Services | ____ | ____ | ____ |
|    a. Classrooms and lecture facilities | ____ | ____ | ____ |
|    b. Computer labs and facilities | ____ | ____ | ____ |
|    c. Science labs and facilities | ____ | ____ | ____ |
|    d. Library and research facilities | ____ | ____ | ____ |

| Exploration Criteria | Very Important | Somewhat Important | Not Important |
|---|---|---|---|
| e. Telecommunication practices (such as remote and hybrid classes) | _____ | _____ | _____ |
| f. Counseling, career services, mental health and related student services | _____ | _____ | _____ |
| g. Services to students with learning challenges and disabilities | _____ | _____ | _____ |
| h. _____ | _____ | _____ | _____ |
| i. _____ | _____ | _____ | _____ |
| 7. Retention, Graduation, and Placement Rates | _____ | _____ | _____ |
| a. Freshmen students returning for sophomore year | _____ | _____ | _____ |
| b. Graduation rate of entering students | _____ | _____ | _____ |
| c. Career placement success of graduates | _____ | _____ | _____ |
| d. Graduate and professional school placement success of graduates | _____ | _____ | _____ |
| e. _____ | _____ | _____ | _____ |
| 8. Size of Undergraduate Student Population | _____ | _____ | _____ |
| a. Large student body (7,500+) | _____ | _____ | _____ |
| b. 5,000–7,499 students | _____ | _____ | _____ |
| c. 2,500–4,999 students | _____ | _____ | _____ |
| d. 1,000–2,499 students | _____ | _____ | _____ |
| e. Small student body (under 1,000) | _____ | _____ | _____ |
| f. _____ | _____ | _____ | _____ |
| g. _____ | _____ | _____ | _____ |

| Exploration Criteria | Very Important | Somewhat Important | Not Important |
|---|---|---|---|
| 9. Location | ___ | ___ | ___ |
| a. Anywhere in the United States | ___ | ___ | ___ |
| b. Anywhere in the region (multistate) | ___ | ___ | ___ |
| c. Anywhere in the state | ___ | ___ | ___ |
| d. Immediate area (75–100 miles) | ___ | ___ | ___ |
| e. Within commuting distance | ___ | ___ | ___ |
| f. Specific location (insert below): | ___ | ___ | ___ |
| 10. Community Environment (setting where college is located) | ___ | ___ | ___ |
| a. Large city (population of 500,000+) | ___ | ___ | ___ |
| b. Medium city (population 100,000 to 499,000) | ___ | ___ | ___ |
| c. Small city (population under 100,000) | ___ | ___ | ___ |
| d. Suburban setting near major urban center | ___ | ___ | ___ |
| e. Small town | ___ | ___ | ___ |
| f. Rural community | ___ | ___ | ___ |
| g. International city | ___ | ___ | ___ |
| 11. Campus and Community Environment | ___ | ___ | ___ |
| a. Student spirit and sense of community | ___ | ___ | ___ |
| b. Friendliness and "feel" | ___ | ___ | ___ |
| c. Student–faculty relationships | ___ | ___ | ___ |
| d. Diverse student population | ___ | ___ | ___ |

| Exploration Criteria | Very Important | Somewhat Important | Not Important |
|---|---|---|---|
| e. Cultural climate | _____ | _____ | _____ |
| f. Social atmosphere/climate | _____ | _____ | _____ |
| g. Security | _____ | _____ | _____ |
| h. Faith-based needs and interests | _____ | _____ | _____ |
| i. Opportunity to participate in the following sport(s): | _____ | _____ | _____ |
| j. Opportunity to participate in the following extracurricular activities: | _____ | _____ | _____ |
| k. Comfortable dormitories | _____ | _____ | _____ |
| l. Healthy and appealing food services | _____ | _____ | _____ |
| m. Comfortable off-campus housing (when and if required) | _____ | _____ | _____ |
| n. Accessible campus (easy to move about) | _____ | _____ | _____ |
| o. Attractive campus and facilities | _____ | _____ | _____ |
| p. Recreational and leisure time activities | _____ | _____ | _____ |
| q. Weekend/social/ entertainment opportunities | _____ | _____ | _____ |
| r. Opportunity to participate in campus or community religious activities | _____ | _____ | _____ |
| s. Health and/or physical facilities | _____ | _____ | _____ |

| Exploration Criteria | Very Important | Somewhat Important | Not Important |
|---|---|---|---|
| t. _____ | ___ | _____ | _____ |
| u. _____ | ___ | _____ | _____ |
| v. _____ | ___ | _____ | _____ |
| 12. College Costs and Student Assistance | ___ | _____ | _____ |
| a. Cost of tuition, room and board, and related costs and fees | ___ | _____ | _____ |
| b. Availability of grants and scholarships | ___ | _____ | _____ |
| c. Availability of loans | ___ | _____ | _____ |
| d. Opportunities for part-time work on campus | ___ | _____ | _____ |
| e. Opportunities for part-time work in community | ___ | _____ | _____ |
| f. _____ | ___ | _____ | _____ |
| g. _____ | ___ | _____ | _____ |

*Chapter 6*

# High School Course Selection

## *Relevance to College Admission*

If there is a single factor that will influence your getting into the college of your choice, it will likely be your record of academic achievement and the quality of the courses in which that achievement was earned. Studies have consistently pointed to a strong academic record in a challenging program of high school preparatory studies as the applicant's strongest ally in the quest for college admission.

All during high school you have been or will be given the opportunity to select or elect courses. This is a point of empowerment in your education, a time when your immediate action can have a significant influence on events in the distant future.

Throughout the high school experience, you should design a challenging curricular experience, one where you are able to address the challenges and graduate with a strong academic record, as reflected in your final grade point average (GPA). In a competitive admission environment, the strength of your academic record could tip the admission scales in your favor. College admission officers know the difference between an advanced level mathematics course and one that requires less study and personal attention.

There are no guarantees or so-called "locks" in the college admission process—even class valedictorians and students with seemingly invincible GPAs are routinely turned down by some highly competitive institutions. It means these colleges are looking for students who have a certain mix of academic and personal characteristics, elements they specifically desire in incoming students. In these situations, criteria other than a strong academic record in a challenging curriculum are influencing the admission formula.

As a rule, competitive or selective colleges want to admit students who have experienced success in a rigorous academic environment and appear capable of continuing that success at the collegiate level. The courses listed here are typical of a strong college preparatory schedule:

- English (four years)
- Science (three to four years, including biology, chemistry, physics, and/or earth science)
- Mathematics (three to four years, including algebra I and II, geometry, trigonometry, and/or calculus)
- History/Social Studies (three to four years)
- Foreign Language (three to four years of the same language)
- Computer Science
- Art and Music

Anyone whose academic abilities allow him or her to participate in Advanced Placement or International Baccalaureate level classes should always do so; those reviewing the admission application will undoubtedly view positively taking such courses. With individual achievement, you should not minimize the importance of courses taken in the senior year—if for no other reason than for the maintenance of a strong work ethic. This is not a time to reduce one's load or cut back on effort.

Consider your education like the conditioning associated with an athletic endeavor. Once a peak level of performance is achieved, you must go into a "maintenance" mode. Otherwise, you will fall out of shape and not be able to sustain the same level of achievement. The so-called senior slump represents a break in conditioning and could result in unnecessary difficulty in college, and, in extreme cases, may even result in the reversal of a previously favorable admission decision.

Think of the college admission formula as a recipe. Most institutions factor the same ingredients into their admission decisions—academic achievement, test scores, teacher or counselor recommendations, and so forth. But, as is often the case with culinary recipes, the chef (in this instance, the college) may rely a bit more or a bit less on a particular ingredient. The main ingredient in most college admission recipes, however, is the level of student performance in a strong curriculum. Translated into simple terms, "study challenging subjects and achieve the best grades possible."

## STUDENT EXERCISE 6.1

### Tracking Your High School Studies

In the space provided below, list the college preparatory courses that you have completed (or plan to complete), ninth grade through senior year:

Ninth Grade or Earlier                                      Grade

_____         _____

_____         _____

_____         _____

Sophomore Year                                             Grade

_____         _____

_____         _____

_____         _____

Junior Year                                                Grade

_____         _____

_____         _____

_____         _____

Senior Year                                                Grade

_____         _____

_____         _____

_____         _____

Summer Study                                               Grade

_____         _____

_____         _____

_____         _____

# Chapter 7

# Learning about College Options

## *Getting the Best Information*

When it comes to gathering information about colleges, students will find an incredible array of sources in a variety of formats. Approach the reference shelf in your local library or the college and career resource center at your high school and you'll find a number of well-used publications that have been placed there to help you. These materials will aid in your general study of colleges and answer the specific questions that you have about particular institutions and their programs. More specific information during this digital age can then be found on institutional websites and social media sites (e.g., Facebook, Twitter, YouTube, etc.).

### USING COLLEGE AND EDUCATION INFORMATION

As you acquire information about colleges, be sure to consider these factors as you evaluate your sources:

- Accuracy—Colleges are changing, dynamic places and you will want to make certain that you're using the latest edition of any publication or information source. Numbers such as those used for dates, amounts, and so on are especially vulnerable and caution should be taken to make sure such information is the most current.
- Variety—Be certain to use a variety of information sources. Some are great for general information; others are better at presenting details. Multiple sources also allow you to perform accuracy cross-checks.
- Bias and misinformation—While the majority of information the student explorer will discover will be factual and accurate, there have been instances over time when content has been biased or distorted by the source. For-profit career, technical and trade institutions have a history

of exaggerating the demand for the occupation and/or their success rate in placing graduates. The basic rule is that if something sounds "too good to be true," it probably requires additional checking

- Information overload—Spread out your exploration activities so that you can consume all that you are learning. Too much information acquired too quickly can lead to confusion and frustration.

## SOURCES OF COLLEGE AND EDUCATIONAL INFORMATION

Information about colleges and other postsecondary education opportunities comes in a variety of forms from a mixture of sources. Use the following information sources in your personal search:

- General college guidance publications—Spend a little time at the beginning of the search examining the general guides and guidebooks—like this one. These resources will help you form questions and structure your college exploration.
- College guides/directories—These are the big, telephone book looka-likes and are produced by publishers such as Peterson's, Barron's, and the College Board. They contain a profile or page on two thousand or more colleges and are great for fact-finding (e.g., college costs, majors, size), but don't judge a college solely by what's in these publications.
- Viewbooks and catalogs—Generated by individual colleges, these publications provide in-depth information about admission criteria, programs of study, student life, and much more. Like most print resources, however, they are slowly being replaced by websites and other digital resources.
- Internet websites—Every college has a website to disseminate admission and financial aid information and communicate with prospective students. Students can access these websites by visiting general Internet search engines like Google, America Online, or Yahoo! and inserting the name of the college after the keyword inquiry. Most colleges allow students to complete their application online and either submit it electronically or print IT out and mail it. Other institutions have created virtual college tours, chat rooms, and electronic newsletters. Further, most have Facebook, Twitter and YouTube sites that offer information useful to prospective applicants and allow them to connect informally to student organizations and campus events and activities. A growing number are offering webinars and other Internet programs to exchange information

with prospective students. Website-driven information has the advantage of being the most current available.

- Virtual tours and webinars—Produced by the colleges, these video programs afford students an opportunity to take a virtual tour of the campus, participate in orientation and information programs, and interact with admission representatives without ever having to leave home.
- Computerized guidance information systems—School-based interactive systems permit students to conduct a guided college search by matching their needs and interests with the offerings of particular colleges.

All of these resources can provide good information that will contribute to quality exploration and sound decision making. They should not, however, be the only sources.

Students can personalize their information quest when they interact with the college admission counselors who visit high schools and participate in local college fair programs. Seize every opportunity to interface with reliable sources.

Finally, as you refine choices, campus visits become a "must" on your exploration agenda. College visits are a reality check of sorts: your firsthand opportunity to see and feel the college . . . to try it on for a "fit." Don't miss it!

Note: The appendix section of the *Bound-for-College Guidebook* contains a comprehensive listing of print and digital resources that are described in the previous pages.

## FREQUENTLY ASKED QUESTIONS

**Question:** How are colleges using social media (Facebook, Twitter, YouTube, etc.) in the admission process?

**Answer:** Colleges created social media accounts for all the reasons anyone else might—they offer a new and innovative venue upon which they can be seen and heard, and where they can also listen. These informal exchanges of information allow the institution to share information quickly and efficiently and reach a growing audience of future students. As a marketing tool, social media sites are extremely beneficial and widely used.

**Question:** I'm told that colleges look at the social media sites of their applicants? What about my social media account could work against me?

**Answer:** As social media site participation grows in the adolescent and young adult population, so has examination of these sites by admission officers.

A Kaplan Test Prep survey in 2021 found 56 percent of the admission staff members regularly visit the social media accounts of their applicants. Given that these sites might help or hurt their application, as well as the fact that they are growing in popularity as a part of application vetting, should be sufficient cause for students to give additional thought to what they post on Facebook, Instagram, Youtube, WhatsApp and TikTok.

Social media sites are great places for you to post profiles and information that describes and defines you. Your site may be the perfect place to profile your interests, talents and achievements, and highlight personal and academic information that isn't asked for in the college application.

Too often, however, the short, cryptic messages that are posted on social media sites are filled with information lacking a certain clarity and completeness that may work against the applicant. Imagine how a college might view a social media account replete with images and words about the parties you attend and the boastful and often exaggerated things that you do. Similarly, imagine that you are applying for need-based financial aid or scholarships and your profile contains picture after picture of you on shopping sprees or your family on lavishly expensive trips. Either could project the wrong "you" and cause the examiner to pause.

Ask yourself if your social media account reflects a true picture of you, the one you would want the college to see if it chose to access your account. Does it contain information about your personal behavior that is questionable and likely to be viewed negatively? If yes, you may wish to revise the message or close your account altogether.

There is one additional social media concern for you to consider. Be wary of offering value opinions on your social media site. If you have spoken about your interest in enrolling at College X more than any other that you have applied to, think about how that message is going to be viewed by College Y and College Z if they happen on to your social media site.

**Question:** When should I request college viewbooks, brochures, and applications?

**Answer:** There really isn't a precise time to begin collecting information about colleges. It will vary from student to student. Start early enough to allow for a thorough search. A good time to become actively engaged in information collection is any time during the junior year. Any earlier and you take the risk that significant information will change before you apply and enroll.

If your choice college requires any examinations, you can indicate on the test form that you want your name and address made available to colleges that will then contact you. Information can also be collected at college fairs and college nights, where you can also interact with admission representatives. While most information contained in college publications remains current, some things (e.g., first year profiles, costs, deadline dates) may change or vary from year to year. When it comes time to apply to college, make sure you have the current college application and follow the current application procedures and submission dates.

**Question:** Are some college guidance tools or resources better than others?
**Answer:** You have probably discovered what other college-bound students have—there are many guides, directories, computer disks, and DVDs purporting to be the best at helping guide you through the college exploration and application process. Several pieces of advice are appropriate here. First, look to the tried and tested college guides and tools, the ones that have been around a few years. Their mere survival attests to their usefulness and quality. Second, ask your counselor or librarian what resources they recommend. Finally, remember to visit colleges and talk with admission representatives. They will complement the information you retrieve from the guides and related tools.

**Question:** There are a number of college video programs in my school's college and career center. Can I learn much by watching them?
**Answer:** Media presentations crashed onto the college admission scene as a part of the information and communication technology revolution of the late 1900's and have been around ever since. Rather than distribute them to places where their use might be limited, colleges today make them available directly on their website.

Most present an accurate and balanced look at the school, offering a visual and audio alternative to all the print resources. Others, however, can be extremely biased, presenting only the parts of the college they want you to see. Counselors have been concerned about the shortage of classroom and instructional scenes as opposed to what appears to be an overload of campus life and social depiction.

**Question:** How can I make sense of all the college information I receive?
**Answer:** If you're receiving a large volume of college literature, you'll want to create a system to keep the information organized. Consider designing a chart that indicates "Name of College," "Date Information Received," and a "Notes" section that will help you evaluate the school. If you haven't received information from a school you want to consider, make a note and contact the school again. Based on your review, start to prioritize your materials, putting the more popular options on the top of the pile. Once you've begun your preliminary exploration, discard the information about colleges you're no longer considering.

**Question:** How can I make the most of a special college night or college orientation program at my high school?

**Answer:** College nights and general information sharing programs for college-bound students at the high school afford you and your parents the unique opportunity of meeting with a number of admission representatives at a single event and getting answers to the questions that are important to you. Like the "prepping" you will do before the larger college fairs, some advance work is in order. Begin by obtaining a list participating colleges from your counselor. Then review their viewbooks and application materials to see what questions these materials might generate. Finally, make a list of the general topics and questions you want to address at the event. Do this homework and you're certain to impress the admission representative.

**Question:** Exactly what is a virtual college fair?
**Answer:** Virtual College Fairs are also a product of the digital communication revolution, the most notable of which are offered by the National Association for College Admission Counseling (virtualcollegefairs.org). NACAC refers to virtual fairs as a dynamic digital meeting space for connecting students and families with colleges and universities.

**Question:** Why don't more admission representatives do in-person visits to my high school?
**Answer:** Colleges assign their admission counselors to in-person visits to high schools according to varying philosophies. Many make certain to visit the schools that traditionally send them students. Others attempt to visit all of the high schools in what they consider to be the area (region or state) where they are best known and are most likely to draw student applications. Still others seek to recruit from a much larger map and will send admission representatives almost anywhere in the nation. However, when the map gets this big, they are not always able to make annual visits. Finally, colleges have been hit by budget restrictions in recent years, and recruiting activities, especially the long-distance trips, have been included in the items being cut or contained. With the money they are not using to travel to high schools, colleges are investing more in digital exchanges.

**Question:** How useful will college guides be in my search?
**Answer:** College guides, the big telephone book lookalikes, have been a staple in the college exploration literature for a very long time. Each contains a page or a column on a particular college and can be used for finding comparative details about costs, location, majors, size, and so on: the kind of information students need to acquire early in the exploration process. The best guides update their information annually and it is crucial that you work with the most current edition. Like other sources of college admission and financial aid information, you should not judge any college solely by what's

in any single publication. However, when considered with other sources and a visit, this information can be very valuable. See examples in Appendix.

## STUDENT EXE) CISE 7.1

### Finding and Using College Guidance Resources

In the space below, keep track of the var us publications, computer disks, social media sites, multi-media programs, d related guidance resources that you use during the college exploration an lecision-making process. Be certain to identify where you found the reso ce (e.g., library, guidance office, college and career center) in case you wis to use it later in the process.

| RESOURCE | LOCATION | | COMMENTS |
|---|---|---|---|
| *Peterson's Guide to Four Year Colleges* | School library | √ | Good reference to general information about colleges |
| | | | |
| | | | |
| | | | |
| | | | |
| | | | |
| | | | |
| | | | |
| | | | |
| | | | |

## STUDENT EXERCISE 7.2

### Human Information Sources: Preparing to Meet College Admission Representatives

In the space provided below, make a list of colleges and universities that you expect to be visiting your school or participating in future college fair programs. Following each institution, write in the specific questions you wish to ask the admission representative(s).

College: _____

Questions: _____

_____

_____

_____

College: _____

Questions: _____

_____

_____

_____

College: _____

Questions: _____

_____

_____

_____

College: _____

Questions: _____

_____

_____

_____

General questions for representatives of all college fair programs: _____

_____

_____

_____

_____

*Chapter 8*

# Using the Internet to Explore and Apply to Colleges

Likely the most powerful tool of the information and communication technology revolution, the Internet has become a valuable and reliable source of information about colleges and a popular mechanism for making application for admission and financial aid online. Every two- and four-year college in the United States has a website.

At these websites students can obtain information about programs of study, admission requirements, college costs, and get answers to frequently asked questions (FAQs) that will guide them in making their college decisions. Students with access to a computer (personal or laptop) with an Internet connection at home or in their school or library should take advantage of this information vehicle and use it throughout the exploration and application process.

While Internet websites will vary remarkably in the breadth of information they offer and their user friendliness, they are usually reliable with respect to both the accuracy and timeliness of the information that is posted there. Prospective students must remember these are public information sites where a college wishes to put forward a positive view of itself. Information gathered from websites, like print and other information, must be evaluated.

Students can access individual college websites often by typing "www."—followed by the name—followed by "edu." Example: www.dickinson.edu will take you directly to Dickinson College's website. Often it is a variation or twist on the name—Shippensburg University's website, for example, can be found at www.ship.edu. Should you fail to access the website by the college name, the next best route is to go through one of the major search engines like www.google.com or www.yahoo.com and use either their education directory or the college name to get you to the institution you wish to explore.

Most college websites offer you a link to the admission or financial aid pages, and here again they vary in both usability and content. Some offer just the basics; others are very sophisticated—[li]ke allowing you to take a virtual tour of their campus, including both visua[l a]nd audio messages.

In addition to institution websites, ther[e] are a number of general Internet locations where students can obtain inform[a]tion and conduct searches of college and financial aid databases. Some of t[he]se sites require student registration which you may or may not wish to do. Wh[e]n you have a little time, visit one of more of the following and do a bit of e[xp]loring:

## GENERAL COLLEGE EXPLORATION

ACT: http://www.actstudent.org/college
Cappex: http://www.cappex.com
College Board: http://www.collegeboard.org
College Insight: http://college-insight.org
College Majors: http://www.collegemajors101.com/
Colleges that Change Lives: https://ctcl.org
College Navigator: http://nces.ed.gov/collegenavigator
College Results Online: http://www.collegeresults.org
Common Application: http://www.commonapplication.org
Education Trust College Results Online: http://www.collegeresults.org/
National Association for College Admission Counseling (Information about tools for college admission and financial aid information and college fairs): http://www.nacacnet.org
Naviance: https://www.naviance.com
Newsweek: https://newsweek.com.rank[...]-best-colleges-america-1162604
New York Times—The Choice: http://thechoice.blogs.nytimes.com
Petersons College Guides: http://petersons.com
Unigo: http://www.unigo.com
U.S. Department of Education College Scorecard: http://collegescorecard.ed.gov/?ltclid=
U.S. News and World Report: https://www.usnews.com/best-colleges

## FINANCIAL AID AND SCHOLARSHIPS

FastWeb Information about Financial Aid and Scholarships: http://www.fastweb.com/college scholarships
FinAid Financial Aid Resources: http://www.finaid.org
National Association of Student Financial Aid Administrators: http://www.nasfaa.org/students/About_Financial_aid.aspx
Project Student Debt: http://projectstudentdebt.org/

Scholarship Care: https:www.scholarshipcare.com/category/scholarship
-for-undergraduate/

U.S. Department of Education College Cost Calculator: http://collegecost.
ed.gov/net-price

U.S. Department of Education Scholarship, Loan and Loan Forgiveness
Information: https://www2.ed.gov/fund/grants-college.html?src=rn

## TESTING AND TEST PREPARATION

ACT: http://act.org/products/k-12-act-test/
College Board: http://sat.collegeboard.org/about-tests
Number 2: www.number2.com

A number of these Internet sites will allow students to submit search criteria (major field of study, size, location, etc.) and narrow their search results. Others offer a wealth of information that can be studied as part of the exploration, decision-making, and application process.

Caution: Internet addresses change from time to time and readers are encouraged to use a good search engine to find the above sources if the link fails.

Once a prospective student has determined the colleges to which he or she wishes to apply, the chances are likely that the institution will allow him or her to apply online. Here again, the application features vary. The colleges out in front in the use of information technology will allow their applicants to complete the admission application, pay fees, and submit essays—all electronically. Most will have variations of these features. Applications for scholarships and financial aid may also be completed and submitted this way.

Finally, students using the Internet to explore and apply can also establish ongoing communication with the colleges that interest them. Many conduct live, interactive webinars, disseminate electronic newsletters, and offer chat rooms for prospective students. They may even connect you with "e-pals," current students with whom you can exchange e-mail correspondence.

If you have mastered the world of electronic communication, add the Internet to your college exploration and application strategies and let cyberspace be one more ally in your information quest.

## FREQUENTLY ASKE) QUESTIONS

**Question:** How successful can I expect be using the Internet to gather information about colleges?

**Answer:** An hour or two browsing the In net spaced over time can lead to a remarkable discovery. Avoid informatio overload by consuming information in reasonable bites. American college nd universities have placed a lot of admission and financial aid informatio on their home pages and each is finding new and innovative ways of usin echnology to tell their story and communicate with prospective students.

In some instances, these websites are re ricted to visual and text presentations, the same information that is curren y contained in viewbooks. Some of the commercial services and publisher are going to try to sell you their products. Others, especially the college a university sites, have added the interactive features that allow you to requ t personal information and inter- act personally with a member of their ad ssion staff. The Internet has cre- ated a unique capability for colleges and u versities to place comprehensive admission information at your fingertips.

## STUDENT EXERCISE 8.1

### Internet Sites That Help with College Exploration and Application

Create and maintain a list of your favorite college admission and financial aid websites and the Internet locations you will want to keep for future reference.

General college exploration and admission websites:

_____

_____

_____

_____

Scholarship and financial aid websites:

_____

_____

_____

_____

Testing and test preparation websites:

_____

_____

_____

_____

Specific college and university websites:

_____

_____

_____

_____

Social media websites with links to colleges and universities:

_____

_____

_____

_____

Virtual college/campus tour websites

_____

_____

_____

_____

*Chapter 9*

# Making the Most of the College Fair Experience

During your high school years, you will most likely have an opportunity to participate in a college fair or a college night program, an event where representatives from a number of colleges and universities gather in one place to meet prospective students and present information about their institutions and programs. Interaction with college representatives allows you to get answers to your personal questions and clarify or correct information that you acquired from other sources.

College fairs come in various sizes and formats. Small events of ten to thirty colleges may be held at your school. Larger fairs are often sponsored by a school district or group of schools and are held in a central location in the community or region. The biggest fairs, attracting hundreds of colleges, are a part of the National College Fair program that is sponsored by the National Association for College Admission Counseling (NACAC) and its affiliates.

The NACAC fairs (www.nacacnet.org) are typically held in large civic centers and are attended by students from a large city or metropolitan area. College fairs come in various sizes and formats. Small events of ten to thirty colleges may be held at your school. Larger fairs are often sponsored by a school district or group of schools and are held in a central location in the community or region. The NACAC fairs (www.nacacnet.org) are typically held in large civic centers and are attended by students from a large city or metropolitan area.

The coronavirus pandemic restrictions regarding social distancing and crowd size forced NACAC to move from in-person fairs to a virtual career fair offering, an action that was met with a certain level of success and expected to be an option for NACAC's national college fairs of the future. The association continues to rethink in-person programming and this ongoing examination may result in both virtual and in-person fairs in the future.

Students can either visit www.nacacnet.org or look to their counselor to learn how NACAC resolves this matter.

College fairs provide you with a unique opportunity to talk directly with admission officers or counselors or with alumni or student representatives who assist the college in its admission efforts. A bit of preparation on your part will allow you to gain more from the experience than if you simply walk into the fair "cold." Such "prep" might include the following:

- Do your college fair homework. Study the list of participating colleges (if available) and prepare a list of questions. Review their literature and visit their websites in advance of the fair. Take your questions to the fair and don't be shy about asking them.
- Participate in as many fairs as are available to gain exposure to the broadest array of colleges and universities. Multiple fair attendances at different times in your high school experience will also allow you to build lessons learned at different exploration points.
- If attending in-person fairs, be prepared to complete many student inquiry cards. To expedite this process, you can prepare preaddressed labels that can be affixed to the college's card or cards with your name and contact information. You may wish to jot down your area of academic interest and any desired information (e.g., viewbook or application request, scholarship criteria, etc.) on the card you leave with the representative.
- Allow sufficient time to talk with as many college representatives as possible. If you are undecided about where to apply, use the fair to continue your exploration. While many colleges will be familiar to you, others will not. If you have narrowed your list of colleges, the fair will permit you to be more focused in your information quest, but you may wish to engage in discussion with some colleges that are not currently on your consideration list. Be open to new information and interface with colleges that are new to you. It's part of the discovery process.
- Allow time to attend the admission and financial aid seminars that may be offered as part of the in-person fair or program. Presented by experts in the field, these seminars offer valuable guidance to aid you in the decision-making and application processes.
- Have a pencil, paper, or a notebook handy and take time to jot down information that you deem important, including answers to your questions. If at an in-person fair, carry a shoulder bag or knapsack as many of the colleges will have information that they wish to leave with you.
- Note the names of the admission representatives with whom you interact and take some time after the fair to write follow-up notes or letters to

those colleges for which you have special questions. Targeted letters get faster responses than the "to whom it may concern" variety.

- Talk with your fellow students after the fair and compare notes regarding the information you received and the impressions that were created. Comparing your insights and experiences with others may generate perspectives that were not apparent before. Your counselor can also help you to digest all of the information you have acquired.
- Present yourself in the best possible manner. The college fair is an opportunity for you to interact face-to-face with college admission representatives, individuals who might eventually be involved in reviewing your application and contributing to the admission decision. Make a powerful first impression with this individual. Just like you jotted down a few points on your inquiry card, the admission representative may have made a few notes about you after you walked away.

College fairs and college day/night programs present the formidable challenge of gathering and managing a lot of information fired at you from different directions by a lot of people in a short period of time. Take some time at the end of the activity to debrief, organize the information you have collected, and consider any impressions the experience had on you.

Note: When preparing for college fairs, complete Student Exercise 7.2, Human Information Sources: Preparing to Meet College Admission Representatives. This information will help you navigate the college fair or college day/night program to your greatest advantage.

## FREQUENTLY ASKED QUESTIONS

**Question:** How can I determine when and where the major college fairs in the nation will be held?

**Answer:** The largest network of national college fairs are the in-person and virtual college fairs sponsored by the National Association for College Admission Counseling. This organization is the most experienced at the design and delivery of these events in major cities and metropolitan areas around the nation. A visit to www.nacacnet.org or a chat with your counselor can provide you with this information. Information about local fairs and the growing number of virtual fairs being offered on the Internet will be known by your counselor.

## Chapter 10

# Campus Visits

## Getting Ready to Go

Choosing a college is more than choosing a place to study and learn. You are also selecting the home where you will live during the next two, four, or maybe more years. Some admission officers express concern that as many as one-fourth of their freshmen students do not step foot on campus until they have arrived to start classes. This lack of hands-on investigation may contribute to the dismal retention statistics at some colleges.

As has been reported various times in this edition of the *Bound-for-College Guidebook*, campus visits are one of the college exploration vehicles that has slowed and, in some instances, stopped due to the social distancing rules set on some campuses and in some communities. When normal conditions return or when smaller groups are doable, participation in campus visits represent a valuable opportunity to see prospective institutions up close and personal. The newly created virtual campus tours and electronic interaction events with admission counselors, while valuable uses of digital communication, fall a tad short of the mark when it comes to walking the campus, sitting in a class, and taking part in an information and orientation event.

To this point your exploration has probably been concentrated on the information that you have been able to gather from guidance resources, your visits to college websites, participation in social media sites, and from interaction with people. As the list gets smaller and your exploration becomes more refined, the remaining colleges merit the scrutiny of a campus visit.

Whether your campus visit will be productive may depend on the tasks that you complete in advance of your departure date. Consider the following:

- Let the admission office know that you're coming. This notice often allows you to visit a class or two, participate in a guided tour, take part in an admission interview (if required) and meet with representatives of the financial aid office. By planning ahead, you may also have

77

an opportunity to stay overnight in   dormitory. If you arrive without notice, these options may not be avai ble to you.

- If you have friends or know alumni f m your school attending the college, arrange to visit with them durin; our visit. Your counselor may be able to identify some students for yo o contact.
- When trying to determine the best t e for a college visit, there are a number of factors to consider. To get e true feel of a college, it is best to visit while it is in session and, the fore, alive with activity. Ideally, you will have refined your choices d be prepared to conduct some visits during the spring of your junic year. If not, set aside some time early in your senior year.
- Some colleges hold open houses or ecial admission-orientation programs. There are pluses and minuses ssociated with these events, and you will need to determine if what y i are trying to find out about the college will be served by your parti pation. The major negative with formal orientation programs is that ou and your fellow visitors get a canned presentation, some of whi will test your ability to sit still and listen.
- Arrange a visit schedule that allows arent or guardian participation. Colleges welcome parental involven nt and often will provide special activities for them.
- Create an itinerary that allows you visit more than one campus on the same trip. Multiple visit itinerarie can be planned using one of the Internet travel sites (e.g., Google Maj , MapQuest). If you are traveling long distances, ask the admission off e if it has arrangements with airlines for discounted student travel far . Take advantage of seasonal and special airfares. The Amtrak rail syst n has a student discount program for ages 17–24 that can be applied to ampus visits travel.
- Make certain that your schedule affor s you not only ample opportunity to visit the college, but also time to eck out the community in which the college is located. Even if you l e the college, you don't want to become a campus "prisoner" or be re iired to exit on weekends to have a reasonable social, recreational, or c tural life.
- Prepare for the visit by making a c cklist of the specific things you want to view and by creating a list c questions you wish to ask. Take your camera along to shoot some inf mal shots of the surroundings to serve as a reminder of the visit.

Remember, you wouldn't buy a jacket o pair of shoes without trying them on first or a car without a test drive. Don' ommit to your collegiate experience without a similar trial. This is your c nce to play detective and get the answers to all of your important questions. se the campus visit approach that you are trying on each college to see "how it fits." It may save you from a day when you look back and say, "I wish I would have known."

Note: Just like your preparation for college fairs, you need to get ready to go on your campus visit with your homework done and your questions ready. Along with Student Exercise 10.1, which follows, you may also want to revisit Student Exercise 7.2, Human Information Sources: Preparing to Meet College Admission Representatives. The information generated by these two exercises will help you make the most of each campus visit.

## FREQUENTLY ASKED QUESTIONS

**Question:** I'm a sophomore. Do you think it's too early to start visiting colleges?

**Answer:** No, but you may have to revisit some colleges when the exploration process heats up in your junior and senior year. Starting early allows the student to engage in a more relaxed and open view of the campus, student body, curriculum, and related matters. Get answers to the questions you have now. Your visits and other aspects of the exploration process are also likely to generate other questions that will have to be answered later. Start a portfolio with a section for every college visited and insert some notes after you return home and have time to debrief.

**Question:** How can I get a behind-the-scenes look at the colleges I'm interested in, not just the standard tour the admission office wants me to experience?

**Answer:** You have several options. First, allow yourself sufficient time to visit both the campus and the community beyond what you get to see on the official tour. Consider connecting with someone on campus who is capable of giving you the insider tour, possibly a friend or recent graduate from your high school who is currently enrolled at the college. If you feel that the admission tour didn't allow sufficient time for examination of any portion of the campus, return to these spots for a second and more thorough examination.

**Question:** I am planning to visit colleges in the near future. How important is it to sit in on a class?

**Answer:** Very important. Although you will probably need to get prior approval from the instructor, you shouldn't pass up the opportunity to sit in on a few classes. You'll get a feel for the academic challenge, teaching methods, and level of student participation. Try to stick around after class and talk with the professor and the students. They can answer your questions and tell you if the class is typical of the college.

**Question:** What should I do if time or expense prohibits me from visiting a distant campus before I make my decision to apply?
**Answer:** This happens more than you would expect. Make a concerted effort to get as much information as you can about the college and be certain that it meets what you're looking for in a college from an academic perspective. Also examine descriptive and demographic information to ensure that it has the things you want to study, is the right size, and meets the other criteria you deem important. It would help to talk with recent graduates or persons you know who also know the college.

If you are admitted before seeing the college, make every attempt to visit before you enroll. Otherwise, college will be somewhat like a blind date. Some are great, others not so great!

**Question:** Should I spend a night on campus and, if so, what should I look for?
**Answer:** An overnight stay will extend the time you have to evaluate the college and determine if it possesses what you are looking for. Many colleges now provide accommodations (housing and meals) for prospective students and their parents. This extra time will also allow you to see the college after hours, during which you might also attend a campus event or spend some time talking with current students. Overnight stays can be very time-consuming if you're attempting to visit multiple campuses, but the time may be well spent.

**Question:** What can I learn by engaging in virtual college/campus tours that are now offered by many colleges?
**Answer:** Many colleges now encourage students and parents, especially those who might otherwise skip or not participate in an "on campus" tour, to conduct that activity via their website. These valuable institution-produced programs, however, are somewhat limiting in content and lack the spontaneity of the live experience.

At the height of the coronavirus pandemic social distancing period, these tours became the only way such tours could be experienced. They remain a popular alternative today.

## STUDENT EXERCISE 10.1

### Preparing for the College Visit

In order for campus visits to be constructive and a valuable use of your time, it is necessary for you to engage in some pre-visit planning. Develop an itinerary and make the necessary contacts to ensure that you see the things you wish to see and get answers to your questions.

College: _____

Contact person: _____ Telephone # _____

Date of visit: _____ Time: _____

Official admission interview: _____ Yes _____ No

People you wish to visit:

| Name | Telephone # | Appointment time | Location |
|------|-------------|------------------|----------|
| _____ | _____ | _____ | _____ |
| _____ | _____ | _____ | _____ |
| _____ | _____ | _____ | _____ |
| _____ | _____ | _____ | _____ |

Questions for admission representatives:

_____
_____
_____
_____

Questions for students on campus:

_____
_____
_____
_____

Questions for faculty members:

_____
_____
_____
_____

Things you want to see on campus:

_____          _____
_____          _____
_____          _____
_____          _____

Things you want to see in college commu ty:

_____          _____
_____          _____
_____          _____
_____          _____

Note: Make a similar list for each college  sit.

# Chapter 11

# Campus Visits

## *Being There and Afterward*

You've arrived on campus. It's bigger than you thought it would be. No, it's smaller. Which buildings are the dorms? Which are the classrooms? There is a buzz of excitement about the campus. It's rather sedate. The students appear friendly. All, some, or none of these impressions may greet you when you make your campus visits, but each contributes to the personality of the college; a personality that you should try to define while you are there.

The mission of your campus visit is twofold. First, you want to get answers to the specific and general questions that you have determined are important to you in your college selection. In some instances, you will be looking for reaffirmation of information that you have acquired from other sources. Second, you are conducting a test or trial of sorts. This up close and personal view of the college—limited as it may be—will allow you to get the feel of the place—to "try it on for fit."

During each visit to a campus, you should attempt to have as many of the following experiences as possible. Otherwise, a return visit may be warranted.

- Sit in on a class or two. If possible, find a class whose subject is of interest to you. While the time will be very short, you can assess the level of student enthusiasm, the degree to which they seem prepared, and some sense of teaching styles.
- Talk with a professor, department chair, or academic advisor. Ask about the academic requirements, program of studies, class size, instructional strategies, and other academic matters. Inform them of your academic experiences in high school and collegiate goals and invite their appraisal or comment.
- Check out the library, computer and science labs and other learning support facilities. If you have particular learning needs, talk with those providing that assistance or service.

- Examine the total living environmen[t] including the dormitories, dining halls, recreational facilities, student c[enter]—all of the places where you will spend time when not in the cla[ss]room. Are these facilities clean, comfortable, and attractive? Do the fa[ci]lities offer privacy when desired? Sample the food and determine if you[r die]tary needs and preferences can be met. Are there places to relax, pla[y] and enjoy some "down time?"
- Talk with students. Let them know th[at] you're considering applying. Do they seem friendly, enthusiastic, and [re]sponsive to your questions? Ask what they would have liked to have k[n]own before enrolling, but didn't.
- Participate in a guided tour. Listen t[o] the guide's presentation and ask questions that it may generate. Take y[o]ur own informal tour. Go back to those places that aroused your curiosi[ty] or where you didn't get to spend enough time. Wander away from the [ca]mpus to see what the community surrounding the college is like.
- If the college requires a personal i[nte]rview as part of the admission process, schedule this activity while [yo]u're on campus. Prepare for the interview, including making a list of q[u]estions you wish to ask. If you're interested in the college, let that inter[est] show!
- Keep your eyes and ears open. Wha[t i]s the general physical condition of the college? Is the campus atmosp[he]re to your liking? Are there lines and crowds? How do students dress[?] Bulletin boards and posters tell many stories about campus life or the [l]ack thereof.
- Take notes. Pick up things (e.g., st[ud]ent newspapers) along the way. Take some pictures. Jot down a fe[w] notes right after the visit while information and impressions are fres[h a]nd clear. Use all of your senses!
- Send thank you notes to any hosts o[r i]ndividuals that took time to help you and answer your questions.

CSI (Crime Scene Investigation) has b[ee]n a popular television series and you are about to be engaged in a persona[l C]SI of sorts, your College Scene Investigation. Look for every clue. Let no [c]orner of the campus escape your study. Question all the "witnesses." Very [so]on you will be refining your list of prospective colleges even more. Each [ca]mpus visit will contribute to the two decisions you will soon be making: w[h]ere to apply and where to enroll if admitted.

## FREQUENTLY ASKE[D] QUESTIONS

**Question:** If an interview is not a part of [th]e college visit itinerary, should I ask for one?

**Answer:** There are several conditions under which you might wish to request an interview. One, if there is any aspect of your educational experience (e.g., death in the family or health problems that affected your academic performance) that can't be conveyed via the application or require detailed explanation, you might want to use a personal interview with an admission officer or counselor to present that information. Second, if you have personal questions that you don't want to ask a college tour guide or feel uncomfortable asking in a group forum, you can request an interview to acquire this information. Basically, you should use any optional strategy whenever you need additional information or think it will strengthen your application.

**Question:** Many colleges include a virtual campus tour on their website. Aren't these as useful as an actual college visit?

**Answer:** While the new technologies are bringing much more to student explorers via the Internet, nothing beats the real thing. A campus visit allows you to see, hear, touch, smell, and yes, even taste a college. For example, virtual tours are often deficient in showing you exactly how large or small the campus really is. They are limited in how much contact you can actually have with students, faculty, and admission and financial aid counselors. And finally, there is no way you can get a taste of dining hall food or observe "up close and personal" a real dormitory room over the Internet.

## STUDENT EXEI :ISE 11.1

### Campus Visit Report Form: Experien s and Impressions

Following each campus visit take a few m nutes to write down your impressions and evaluate the experience. Also j : down any remaining questions or concerns that need to be addressed if y are to keep this college on your prospect list. After you have completed l of your college visits, put the report forms side by side and compare the nformation contained on each.

College: _____ Dat visited: _____

Check each of the activities you experienc d and places you visited:

_____ Campus tour (guided)          _____   brary
_____ Campus tour (on your own)    _____   omputer, science, and
                                                                 lated labs
_____ Class observation(s)              _____   creational facilities
_____ Student interview(s)              _____   hletic event
_____ Professor interview(s)           _____   oncert, play, or cultural event
_____ Admission                            _____   ampus store
          officer interview
_____ Financial aid                        _____   ommunity tour
          officer interview
_____ Dormitory                          _____   ning hall
_____ Student union/                    _____   her (specify _____)
          campus center

Special Experiences—Did you experience ny of the following?

Observe a college class or classes: _____ Y ; _____ No

If yes, what were your impressions?

_____          _____
_____          _____
_____          _____
_____          _____

Meet with professors or other staff membe s: _____ Yes _____ No

If yes, what were your impressions?

_____

_____

_____

_____

Meet with students: _____ Yes _____ No

If yes, what were your impressions?

_____

_____

_____

_____

Stay overnight in a dorm: _____ Yes _____ No

If yes, what were your impressions?

_____

_____

_____

_____

Read the college newspaper or examine the items posted on the student union bulletin board: _____ Yes _____ No

If yes, what were your impressions?

_____

_____

_____

_____

Take a walk or ride around the community in which the college is located: _____ Yes _____ No

If yes, what were your impressions?

_____

_____

_____

_____

Note: Make additional copies of this report form for each college visit.

## STUDENT EXEI ISE 11.2

### Evaluating the College Visit

Rate your impression of the following a demic, student life, and related elements as experienced or observed du g your campus visit. Circle the number that best reflects your impressio If other features influenced you favorably or unfavorably, list the items in ne of the vacant spaces and rate it accordingly.

| College | Rating Favorable to Unfavorable | | | | |
|---|---|---|---|---|---|
| Academic climate and competition | 5 | 4 | 3 | 2 | 1 |
| Student spirit and enthusiasm | 5 | 4 | 3 | 2 | 1 |
| Friendliness and geniality | 5 | 4 | 3 | 2 | 1 |
| Class size | 5 | 4 | 3 | 2 | 1 |
| Instructional style | 5 | 4 | 3 | 2 | 1 |
| Instructional facilities/classrooms | 5 | 4 | 3 | 2 | 1 |
| Library, laboratories, and support facilitic | 5 | 4 | 3 | 2 | 1 |
| Student services and special programs | 5 | 4 | 3 | 2 | 1 |
| Living and social facilities | 5 | 4 | 3 | 2 | 1 |
| Dorms | 5 | 4 | 3 | 2 | 1 |
| Dining hall | 5 | 4 | 3 | 2 | 1 |
| Student union/center | 5 | 4 | 3 | 2 | 1 |
| Size of college | 5 | 4 | 3 | 2 | 1 |
| Student composition and diversity | 5 | 4 | 3 | 2 | 1 |
| Location of the college | 5 | 4 | 3 | 2 | 1 |
| Campus atmosphere and environment | 5 | 4 | 3 | 2 | 1 |
| Church, cultural, and related opportunitie | 5 | 4 | 3 | 2 | 1 |
| Fitness facilities (gym/pool/running trail: | 5 | 4 | 3 | 2 | 1 |
| Community environment | 5 | 4 | 3 | 2 | 1 |
| Social life/extracurricular activities | 5 | 4 | 3 | 2 | 1 |
| Online and remote class capability | 5 | 4 | 3 | 2 | 1 |

General observations:

_____
_____
_____
_____

Note: Make additional copies of this report form for each college visit.

# Chapter 12

# Admission Plans

## *Modes of Admission Access*

When the time arrives to apply to a college or university, the student will find that institutions offer a number of plans for the submission of applications. Depending where you are in your personal exploration and decision making, one of these plans may suit your particular application requirements. Review and consider all admission plan options. Consult with your school counselor or the admission counselor at the specific college if you have any concerns or questions.

Students and parents would be well advised to study the NACAC Guide to Ethical Practices in College Admission (nacacnet.org) which offers details about the various modes of admission access and how the organization believes its members should conduct their relationships with students applying for admission and financial aid. All students should know that NACAC subscribes to the National Candidates Reply Date, a date widely recognized as May 1. This is the time when students should be asked for confirmation of offers of admission, financial aid, housing and other enrollment matters.

This NACAC Guide also contains numerous definitions of admission terms and expressions that are worthy of attention by the student explorer. Taken directly from the NACAC document, the following passages provide such details:

## APPLICATION PLANS

Non-restrictive application plans: Colleges allow students who are filing out applications using one of these non-restrictive plans to submit applications to multiple institutions. It is recommended that colleges allow students who are offered enrollment using one of these plans until at least May 1 to confirm their intent to enroll. Colleges should disclose whether admission to their institution or to any of their programs or r jors or selection for scholarships is on a first-come, first-served basis.

- Early Action (EA): Students apply l an earlier deadline to receive a decision in advance of the college's l gular Decision notification date.
- Regular Decision (RD): Students su iit their applications by a speci-fied deadline and are notified of a lecision within a clearly stated period of time.
- Rolling Admission (RA): Students ply at any time after a college begins accepting applications until final closing date, which may be as late as after the start of the t m for which they are applying. Students are notified of a decision a their applications are completed and are reviewed.

Restrictive application plans: Colleges ilizing one of these plans restrict the applications that students can file with ther institutions.
- Early Decision (ED): Students comi t to a first-choice college at the time of application and, if admitted, ree to enroll and withdraw their other college applications. Colleges iy offer ED I or II with different deadlines. Students may be required t accept a college's offer of admis-sion and submit a deposit prior to Ma 1.

Colleges using an Early Decision applic ion should

- Not make Early Decision the only ap ication option for admission.
- Notify candidates of the admission lecision within a clearly stated period of time.
- Respond to an application for financi aid at or near the time of an offer of admission and before a deposit is quired.
- Release applicants from the Early De sion agreement if the candidate is denied admission, deferred to an adm sion date other than that stated on the original application, or offered a rogram or major that is different from that stated on the original appli tion.
- State any admission preferences for s cific applicant populations, such as legacies (typically siblings or the c spring of alumni/ae) or recruited athletes.
- State if admission preferences are ailable only to Early Decision candidates.

Restrictive/Single Choice Early Action EA): Students apply to a college of preference and receive an admission d ision in advance of the Regular

Decision notification date. Colleges may place certain restrictions on applying under other early application plans.

- Students admitted under Restrictive Early Action should be allowed until May 1 to accept the college's offer of admission or to submit a deposit.
- Colleges with Restrictive/Single Choice Early Action should not restrict students from applying under other colleges' Regular or Rolling application plans.
- Colleges should clearly articulate their restrictions in their Restrictive/ Single Choice Early Action policies and agreements with students.
    (Source: NACAC Guide to Ethical Practices in College Admission, 2020)

The various admission plans presented require study in order for the student to determine which one fits best. For example, students dependent on a financial aid offer may not want to commit to applying for an early decision as it will require a commitment they may not wish to make until multiple aid offers are received and considered. If you're still in the process of exploring and considering options, using the Regular Decision plan is probably the best course of action.

## ADMISSION PROTOCOLS AND PROCEDURES UNDER SCRUTINY

Always under examination and study by the colleges and universities that use them, admission protocols and procedures in the past few years have been placed under a larger microscope by the global coronavirus pandemic tragedy and the shocking headlines brought to light during the Varsity Blues Scandal. Institutions have reacted promptly by creating a "new normal" when it comes to the business of admitting and screening students. Future students must be sensitive to how these practices have changed and react accordingly. Again, the counselor and admission officer can be your best allies during these times of change.

## FREQUENTLY ASKED QUESTIONS

**Question:** What are the circumstances under which an "early" application might be appropriate?
 **Answer:** Early action, early decision, and restrictive early action plans were created to help the informed and committed student who is ready to apply and

they allow the applicant to bring closure to the application process earlier in the senior year. On the negative side, early plans are not always the best direction to take if the student has a high level of financial need and requires additional time to negotiate an attractive financial aid package. In these instances, it may be wise to apply to multiple colleges and compare financial aid offers. Finally, don't apply early just to be done with the process or because you hear it is the best way to get in. It has to be right for you. Your counselor and the admission representative at the college can provide information about the nuances of any particular early plan.

**Question:** Do all the early plans follow the same guidelines and calendar?
**Answer:** No. While much of the admission process is moved forward, not all colleges want you to act in a uniform manner. Students need to be sensitive to institutional variables and follow precisely the guidelines and calendars of that college's early plan.

**Question:** Does an application to an early plan have a greater chance of resulting in an acceptance?
**Answer:** Just because the number of applicants to early plans will be fewer than those applying via regular admission plans, one cannot assume there will be less competition. Most colleges apply more stringent criteria to students applying early. Further, each institution has a different philosophy on how they scrutinize early applications and the number of applicants they will admit under such a plan. Any school counselor experienced in working with college-bound students can be a great sounding board as to whether your academic achievements and personal characteristics make you a viable early notification, action, or decision candidate. Seek counsel!

*Chapter 13*

# Degree of Difficulty

## *Understanding the Admission Competition*

Will I be accepted? That's the question that you have probably asked yourself a hundred times as you look at colleges and consider applying for admission. According to a recent reporting of a study conducted annually by the Higher Education Research Institute at UCLA, 55 percent of college freshmen surveyed said they were attending their first-choice college. Another 28 percent indicated it was their second choice.

Good exploration, sound decision making, and adherence to a rigorous schedule of admission and financial aid application tasks are three of the reasons more than eight in ten first-year students say they are in their first or second choice college. It's important to note, however, that the percentage saying they were accepted at their top choice college has been slipping in recent years and is currently at the lowest point since the survey was initiated in 1974.

As you refine your options and move in the direction of making application, you need to evaluate your prospects of acceptance at the college or colleges that you have determined are right for you. When it comes to the consideration of your application, colleges fall into one of several competitive categories. Understanding these categories will help you to file applications that improve your chances of being admitted.

## COLLEGE CATEGORIES

### SELECTIVE COLLEGES

The great majority of colleges and universities are selective, meaning that they require students to meet specific selection criteria in order to be considered for admission. The rigor will vary, but students that match or exceed the criteria stand the best chance o admission.

## COMPETITIVE COLLEGES

When more students apply than the colle can accommodate, the result is heightened competition for limited space The more applications filed with an institution—the more competitive it w be to gain admission. There are many stories about Ivy League colleges th reject the applications of dozens of valedictorians each year. You probably now some very capable students who weren't admitted to highly competiti colleges. If you're a valid candidate for admission to such colleges, yo should consider filing at three or four different colleges to increase your ch ces of admission to one of them.

## OPEN ADMISSION COLLEGES

Open admission colleges, like communit colleges and technical institutes, invite applications from interested student possessing a high school diploma or its equivalent and admit most of the udents that apply. Admission to specific programs (e.g., nursing, technol y, etc.) within these institutions, however, may require more stringent crite .

Students that successfully complete thei high school's college preparatory program are likely to be admissible to mar colleges. Remember, even if you are denied admission to a college, you ha other avenues to the same goal. Don't be afraid to try to be admitted.

## UNDERSTANDING INSTITUTIONAL SELECTIVITY AND COMPETITIVENESS

How do you determine the selectivity o competitiveness of the colleges you're exploring? Consider the following:

1. Examine the characteristics of the tudents the college is currently admitting, the students that you'll competing with in class each day. This information is contained the annual first year class pro file—a composite of the academic mographics of the most recently admitted class.
2. Review the application, acceptance and enrollment statistics of the most recently admitted class. How any applied? How many were accepted? How many actually enrol d. This information is published

in many of the general college guidebooks. If you can't find it, ask an admission representative for the statistics.

3. Talk with students and former students of the colleges. They know first-hand what the academic climate is like. Ask counselors, teachers, and admission officers. They've worked with students who have preceded you and enrolled at the same institutions you are considering.

4. Examine the retention statistics. Many college graduates earned their degrees at colleges that they found after they experienced academic difficulty at their first college. The reasons for transferring can vary (e.g., living and social issues, financial, etc.), but you should never invite academic difficulty by trying to gain admission to a college where your prospects for success are not reasonable.

This information, coupled with a realistic assessment of your personal abilities and interests, can point you toward colleges where you are most likely to be accepted and, more important, be successful. Your goal is to find a college or colleges where you have the greatest chance of enjoying academic achievement in a satisfying living environment. Aspire to succeed and don't invite failure by attempting to get into any college where you won't be successful.

## FREQUENTLY ASKED QUESTIONS

**Question:** Why do students who have been accepted at their first-choice college elect to go to other schools?
**Answer:** There could be a number of reasons, but affordability is likely to have something to do with it. In some instances, students with demonstrated need were accepted by their top choice college, but the financial aid package offered didn't meet their demonstrated need. The result is the student is left with no choice other than to go to a less expensive institution or one that is able to offer more in the way of merit-based and need-based aid.

**Question:** Exactly what does it mean when a college is described as selective or competitive?
**Answer:** These terms relate directly to your chances of being admitted to a particular college or how your qualifications compare with other applicants and admitted students. Most colleges and universities require that prospective students meet specific selection criteria. These institutions are known as being "selective." If students meet these criteria, they are likely to be admitted. The term "competitive" is used when there are more qualified candidates than the college can accommodate, resulting in heightened competition for limited

spaces. The more applicants denied admi ion, the greater the competition. If you conduct a realistic assessment of y r personal academic abilities and interests in light of what the college is loo ng for, you can apply to colleges where you are most likely to be accepted.

**Question:** I have some reservations abou ny ability to meet the scholastic requirements at one or two of the colleges  my list. How can I determine if I'm academically qualified to do the work

**Answer:** Your best bet is to discuss your  t of colleges with your counselor and the teachers who know both you and tl colleges you're examining. After that, take a look at the academic profile  the most recent first year class admitted to the college. How do your aca mic qualifications compare with those of the students with whom you will  competing? Finally, discuss your scholastic record with admission counselo and students at the college. One or more of these sources will help you asse  your qualifications and help you decide whether to apply.

**Question:** What is the best way to gair idmission to one of the service academies?

**Answer:** From the very beginning, you n d to understand that the nation's military service academies are among the iost selective of the nation's col- leges, and not only on the basis of acad iics. The service academies are looking for a special kind of student, on who is willing to make a career commitment to serve in one of the ar d forces following graduation. Applicants must be top-notch students,  physically fit, and possess the qualities of leadership found in a military ficer.

Applicants must receive an official non iation to the academy, the major- ity of which are made by members of C( gress for students who reside in their state or congressional district. You ( 1 obtain information about other nomination categories from your counse r or the admission office at the academy that you would like to attend.

*Chapter 14*

# Admission Tests

## *How They Are Used and Strategies for Preparation*

A student once said that the two most anxiety-provoking acronyms in the English language were SAT (Scholastic Aptitude Test) and ACT (American College Test), representing the standardized admission instruments or tests administered respectively by the College Board and ACT. The most commonly utilized tests are the Preliminary SAT/National Merit Scholarship Qualifying Test (PSAT/NMSQT), SAT, PLAN, ACT Assessment, and the Test of English as a Foreign Language (TOEFL). Students engaged in the more challenging academic curricula will also need to know about Advanced Placement (AP) and International Baccalaureate (IB) exams associated with college admission.

### SAT/PSAT

The SAT is a standardized admission or entrance tests and represents one of the criteria that many colleges use in making their admission decisions. The SAT measures a student's reasoning aptitude in an academic context. The PSAT/NMSQT is the practice test for the SAT and taken by juniors. The SAT has three major sections: mathematics, reading, and writing (including an essay). The SAT is typically taken in the junior year and again in the senior year.

These tests are owned, developed and administered by College Board and their website (www.collegeboard.com) is the best information about them.

## ACT ASSESSMENT

The ACT Assessment is the other primary admission test used by colleges in determining the strengths of the applicants for admission. It includes four curriculum-driven (English, mathematics, reading, and science) tests and an optional essay section. This test has been designed to measure the student's general educational development and her or his ability to meet the challenges of the collegiate academic experience. The PLAN is the practice test for the ACT Assessment. Additional information about the ACT exams can be found at www.act.org.

## ADVANCED PLACEMENT AND INTERNATIONAL BACCALAUREATE EXAMINATIONS

The student who has participated in college-level courses in high school may elect to participate in one or more of the many Advanced Placement (AP) examinations offered by College Board (http://www.collegeboard.com/student/testing/ap/about.html) or the International Baccalaureate (IB) examinations administered by International Baccalaureate Organization (www.ibo.org). Successful scores on these challenging exams can lead to earned college credit or advanced standing in collegiate classes after enrollment.

## ROLE OF ADMISSION TESTING IN ADMISSION DECISIONS

As stated earlier in this guidebook, admission testing is one of the factors that many colleges and universities will use in determining admission of applicants. The operative words above are "one" and "many." Numerous studies—repeated over time—suggest that academic achievement in a strong curriculum is the most influential of the various admission factors, but even a 4.0 grade point average isn't always a guarantee. Your GPA and test scores, along with a number of other factors (e.g., class rank, essay, recommendations, extracurricular activities, interview, etc.) are mixed together into an institutional admission formula that guides admission officers.

You should also know that a growing number of colleges, even institutions with reputations for being highly competitive in their admission decisions, have chosen to abandon SAT and ACT test scores as an entrance requirement or make them optional. Your counselor should have a list of those schools or you can visit the National Center for Fair and Open Testing (FairTest) at www.fairtest.org/optinit.htm and get a current list of institutions where admission tests are not required or where they are considered optional.

Your counselor possesses valuable information about which tests you should take, when it is best to take them, when they should be repeated (if necessary), and the process you must follow to properly register for each examination. Both ACT and College Board set examination dates months in advance of their administration and you need to schedule your personal participation at a time convenient to you.

The important thing is to give admission tests their appropriate attention. Too much attention may mean rising anxiety that often results in the distortion of the importance of the tests. Too little attention means that you have failed to recognize the role of these standardized tests in the admission process and your responsibilities in preparing for them. Aim for balance.

## GETTING READY FOR THE EXAMINATION

Can you prepare? Do test prep courses work? Are test prep guides and computer software programs useful? How much will my scores improve? The following tips will guide you in your test-preparation and test-taking experiences:

1. Pursue the most challenging studies possible all during the high school experience. A prophetic counselor once stated that you can't cram into eleven weeks what you should have learned in eleven years of school.
2. Read as much as you can. Whether study related or just for fun, reading is a habit that will pay dividends on test day.
3. Participate in extracurricular activities that are an extension of the classroom experience, such as activities that will enhance your language and mathematics knowledge and skills.
4. Acquire and review any old test editions or practice tests offered by ACT or College Board or visit their student test prep or help sites online. Many testing experts believe your best preperation lies in becoming comfortable as a test taker and familiar with the testing instruments. What better experience than to take a number of practive tests like those posted on www.numbertwo.com? Your counselor may direct you to others.
5. If your scores aren't where you'd like them to be, consider taking the test again or taking the other test (SAT to ACT and vice versa). Talk with your counselor about retesting.
6. For some students, a test prep course may be in order. These tutoring sessions are available from your school and/or commercial test prep

firms. You may also wish to use t... test prep manuals, videos, and computer software materials that ha... been created to improve scores. Before enrolling in a test prep class ...r acquiring these tools, seek the recommendation of your counselo...r students who have used the materials. The bottom line is not to ...pect miracles, and don't fall for outrageous claims of score escalatio...

As the formal test date approaches, rela... and take the experience in stride. Get plenty of rest before the test and car... some nourishment with you on test day to consume during the schedule... breaks. Admission testing is an important event, but it's not the "life and ...ath" experience that some build it up to be.

Test scores alone won't get you in or k... p you out of the vast majority of colleges. Good scores will only enhance y...ur prospects for admission if the other criteria have been met. Low scores ...y cause the admission officer to look for an explanation or deeper into the ...her admission requirements.

## FREQUENTLY ASKED QUESTIONS

**Question:** Which will count more—my h... h school grades or my admission test scores?

**Answer:** Every college has its own formu... for making admission decisions and most will tell you that achievement ... college preparatory studies will weigh more heavily in their decision. Stud... conducted over time have found that colleges requiring them are likely to h...ve defined the role they will play in admitting students, a reasonable questi... to pose for a college admission representative.

Recent times have seen both a permane... or temporary movement to "test optional" status by significant numbers o... nstitutions. FairTest has posted a list of those colleges and universities at ht... ://fairtest.org/.

**Question:** I did not do well on my admis... on tests. To what extent will my low scores keep me out of the college I w... t to attend?

**Answer:** You appear to have already d...ermined that your scores won't get you into the colleges you're consid... ing. Don't give up so quickly! Admission test scores are just one of the ...riteria considered by colleges as they make admission decisions. Promote ...ur strengths as they may be the elements your choice college is looking f... in future students.

Test scores are important to those insti... tions requiring them, but not as important as your achievement in college ... eparatory studies and the rigor of the curriculum you studied. If you truly be... ve your scores are not reflective of the type of work you have done or are capable of doing, attach a note to your application that presents your case and ask your counselor to mention it in his or her recommendation.

**Question:** How does one select a test-preparation program?

**Answer:** Choosing a test-preparation course is best done by obtaining the firsthand evaluation of students who have participated in the programs. Increasingly schools and school districts are offering quality test prep programs for free or for fees far below their for-profit competition. Because most of the commercial test prep firms make similar, and often exaggerated, claims about how much they will improve your scores, try to base your choice on factors such as teaching approach, time commitment, and cost. Look for a program that fits your particular need, learning style, and schedule. Ask the test prep company if you can observe one of its classes before making a final commitment. Finally, remember that a number of self-help publications and software programs provide similar instruction. You may find some of these materials in your school or community library.

**Question:** How can I learn everything ACT and College Board want me to know about admission tests?

**Answer:** Visit the following two websites designed for college-bound students.

ACT: http://www.actstudent.org/college/

College Board: http://www.collegeboard.org

At these sites, the student can learn about dates, formats (print and digital), and other details.

**Question:** Should I retake the admission test if I receive low scores?

**Answer:** Like so many aspects of the college admission process, this is a very individual matter and a general response to your question is difficult. If you truly believe that you can do better, by all means register and take the test again. If the colleges you are applying to accept either test, you may also wish to take the other test (ACT vs. SAT or vice versa). Whatever your personal decision, don't allow the improvement of your test scores to become an obsession, one that generates undue stress and affects your academic progress in a negative manner. Your school counselor may have some valuable guidance on the retake issue. Talk to her or him.

## STUDENT EXEF ISE 14.1

### Creating Your Admission Test Sched e

Meet with your counselor and consult the dministration calendars for those tests that you wish to take as a part of you preparation to apply for college. Make certain you register in accordance th deadlines and meet any other requirements. As you complete each te: and receive the results, update this form.

| Test | Date | Completed | Results received | Forwarded to college(s) |
|------|------|-----------|------------------|-------------------------|
|      |      |           |                  |                         |
|      |      |           |                  |                         |
|      |      |           |                  |                         |
|      |      |           |                  |                         |
|      |      |           |                  |                         |

*Chapter 15*

# Admission Essays

## *Putting Forth Your Best Effort*

How important is the essay? How does the college use the essay in making admission decisions? Like most other admission criteria, the weight given to the essay will vary from institution to institution. However, if the college requires an essay, you must treat it with importance and use it as an opportunity to strengthen your application for admission.

A great deal of the college application process is controlled by the questions asked by the college in its application and your ability to answer those questions in a manner that suggests that you're the kind of student they are seeking to admit. They ask. You answer.

Your opportunities to be creative in your response to the college application process are somewhat limited. If the college requires or recommends an interview, you will be able to put a face and a personality with the application, academic transcript, and test scores. The essay or writing sample requirement will call upon the applicant to analyze an issue or subject, organize thoughts and ideas and then communicate them in a scholarly message.

Like the interview, the essay seeks to learn more about the applicant than can be derived from the formal application questions. More than just a measure of your writing abilities, it also provides insight into your intelligence, expressiveness, and thinking skills. Like the interview, the essay provides you with an opportunity to answer unasked questions and to communicate directly with the educators and officials who have a voice in your admission.

## PREPARING YOUR BEST ESSAY OR WRITING SAMPLE

In preparing the essay that accompanies your college application, consider the following:

1. Talk to college students you know about their essay writing experiences and the subjects about which they were asked to write. This will provide some sense of the challenge you'll find before you.
2. Set aside some specific time to organize your thoughts and do the actual writing and editing of the essay. And times when school and social activities are extremely demanding. The summer after your junior year or the early part of the senior year is the best time to tackle this project.
3. Make certain that you understand the essay assignment directions (e.g., length, word count) and respond appropriately. Some topics are open-ended and allow you reasonable freedom in shaping your response. Others are more structured and ask you to address a specific issue or topic.
4. If the essay is autobiographical, begin by developing an audit of your relevant personal traits and experiences. Be reflective without being boastful.
5. Follow the practices that have worked for you in writing essays, compositions, and research papers in high school:
   • Develop an outline
   • Follow guidelines (if offered)
   • Determine the best format to present your message
   • Prepare a draft
   • Review and edit the draft for grammar, spelling, punctuation, and word usage
   • Evaluate your writing style and treatment of the topic
   • Rewrite and edit as necessary
   • Type, proofread, and prepare for submission
6. Critique your final draft. Did you address the topic? Were you thorough? Did you provide the proper details? Does it flow well? Is it interesting and focused? Does it hold the reader's attention throughout? Have you conveyed your personal position or feelings about the topic?
7. Ask others for their impressions of your draft essay, but do not ask them to write or rewrite your essay. The essay is to be an example of your creativity and the work needs to come from you.
8. Essays are read by human beings, people who read hundreds (or thousands) of essays. Be sure that yours "reader friendly."
9. If the essay is being written under any testing protocols or where a time limitation is imposed, allow sufficient time for proofreading the essay before submission.

College essay readers are looking for thoughtful and sincere content, creative expression, and good writing technique. When you've reached that point, put down your pen, or back away from the keyboard. You have a quality essay!

## FREQUENTLY ASKED QUESTIONS

**Question:** What is the most common mistake applicants make in writing their admission essay?
**Answer:** Too many essay writers read too much into the assignment. They attempt to prepare an essay they think the reader wants to read. Be yourself—be original and you will prepare an excellent essay.

**Question:** Several colleges I'm considering have requested an essay. Why do they have this requirement and how will the essay influence my chances of admission?
**Answer:** While the essay is first a measure of your writing abilities, it also provides the college with insight into your intelligence, expressiveness, and thinking skills. Like the interview, the essay provides you an opportunity to answer unasked questions and to communicate directly with the educators and officials who have a voice in your admission. View the essay as an avenue to admission, not an obstacle.

**Question:** Can you give me some tips on writing the college essay?
**Answer:** Follow the practices that have worked for you in writing essays, compositions, and research papers in high school. Begin by setting aside some quiet time to organize your thoughts and perform the actual writing and editing of your essay. Be certain you understand fully the essay assignment and directions. Carefully proofread your work for grammar, spelling, word usage, and punctuation and critique it for content, thoroughness, detail, and flow. And finally, you may wish to have your parents or a friend read the essay for clarity and completeness.

**Question:** If the admission essay is optional, should I submit one?
**Answer:** Anything "optional" in the college application requirements should be weighed carefully. If you feel that submitting an essay will strengthen your overall application or give the admission officer or committee an opportunity to see a piece of you that is not visible in the remainder of the application, then you would be wise to submit the essay. However, if you don't feel that submitting an essay would influence your application positively, then it's best to exclude it.

*Chapter 16*

# Narrowing Options

## *Deciding Where to Apply*

You've engineered an effective exploration campaign and now know a whole lot more about the colleges you're considering and the educational opportunities they present. Along the way some new colleges were added to the list. Some were removed.

Given the extensive number of four- and two-year colleges and universities and vast network of career, technical and vocational study programs, students wishing to engage in postsecondary education have many options to choose from. Add the possibilities of Internet study and distance education to the mix and even more options will be available.

For the purposes of exploration, you are likely to have placed a relatively small number of these institutions under your personal microscope. That intense examination has produced a refined list of colleges and universities. Now you must study that list (possibly narrowing it even more) and begin the formal application phase of the high school to college transition.

At this point, a number of new questions emerge. How many applications should I submit? What do the colleges need to know about me in order to consider my candidacy for admission? What are my chances of admission? What is the admission competition like this year? Are there ways that I can increase the odds that I will be admitted?

Review the refined list with respect to those factors that you deem important in the selection of your college. Two rules should guide this final review:

Rule Number One—Your objective has not been to find a single college, but rather the colleges that meet your selection criteria. Surely, you have your favorite or favorites, but try not to be so exclusive in this refinement process that you omit viable options. In other words, there is no solitary "right" college; there should be a number of right colleges.

Rule Number Two—Don't apply to any college that you would not attend if offered admission. If the exploratio process has taught you anything, it should have helped you to define y ur educational goals and how the various colleges measure up to the cr ria that you feel are important.

You can address Rule Number Two by a wering the following questions: Is the college the right place for me to le n? Will I feel comfortable there as a student and member of the campus c munity? How is my application going to stack up against all of the others t college will be receiving? Is the college affordable or will the financial aid ffered make it affordable? If the answer to these questions is yes, move the ollege forward on your consideration list. If no, consider removing it.

## FILING MULTIPLE ADMISSION APPLICATIONS

Counselors and admission officers recomm nd that you file multiple college applications, but they do not always agree n the number. Most suggest that three to five applications will be sufficient vary your exposure and enhance your chances of admission to more than o college.

Those institutions should include (1) "s e" colleges where you are highly likely to gain admission, (2) "probable" lleges where you have about a 50–50 chance of admission, and (3) "rea " colleges where admission will depend on the level of competition that pa icular year.

Many students file a single application d are successful. Some file many more than the number suggested above. A ecent survey by UCLA's Higher Education Research Institute revealed the llowing: one application submitted (11%), 2–5 (41%), 6–9 (39%) and mo than 10+ (9%).

Your need for financial assistance ma dictate that you file additional applications to expose your academic qu ifications to a broader range of colleges and the aid options they present. emember, too, that there are fees associated with each college application a filing frivolous applications can be expensive.

You will improve your chances of adm ssion by applying to institutions whose admission standards and require ents mesh with your academic qualifications and personal characteristic This is the admissibility factor and means you profile the kind of stude the college has admitted in the past and is likely to admit in the future. D ote the appropriate commitment and energy to considering all of these co erns. You will be satisfied with the results.

## FREQUENTLY ASKED QUESTIONS

**Question:** What do most students say influenced them most in selecting a college?

**Answer:** A recent National Institute of Education (NIE) survey found the following factors topping the list of things students considered "very important" in choosing their college: Academic quality/ reputation (74%), Offering desired major/program of study (74%), Job placement after study (73%), Cost of attendance (67%) and Graduate school placement after study (58%). While concerns about affordability and incurring debt have been on the rise in recent years, the top of the list has remained constant over time.

**Question:** I've learned a great deal about the right reasons for selecting and making application to a college. What are some of the wrong reasons?

**Answer:** There are a ton of wrong reasons students employ in the admission process. For example, until you have explored all of the options and been rejected for the needed financial assistance, selecting a college based on its lower price tag may be a serious mistake. Let the college know your personal economic situation and see what it can do for you, but don't dismiss it from consideration until all options are considered.

Applying to a college because your girlfriend or boyfriend is applying there or because you have a lot of high school friends there can also produce disastrous results. The same is true for applying to a school where your parents or other family members may have studied. A college that is or was right for them may do absolutely nothing to respond to your academic and career study objectives. Finally, selecting a college based on its having a highly ranked athletic football team, its location in a particular city or region, or its listing in one of the ranking magazines could spell future doom. Identify the colleges that are right for you and apply to them.

**Question:** With so many colleges to choose from, how is it possible to narrow my choices to just one?

**Answer:** For the purposes of applying, you don't have to narrow your choices to just one. And you would be ill advised to do so. Your task is to find a number of places to continue your education in an environment that is comfortable and suitable to your needs. Admission to a college that is right for you may require that you apply to multiple institutions. Begin early creating a list of things that you are looking for in your future college. Revise the list as your views change and other things become important to you. Hold up all of the colleges you examine to these criteria. Soon a list of suitable colleges will begin to emerge.

Students may wish to consider using he Equitable Value Explorer, a user-friendly website where they can eval te more than 4,000 colleges and universities on a variety of factors. This to grew out of the work of the Bill and Melinda Gates Foundation's Postseco dary Value Commission and can be found at https://equity.postsecondaryva e.org.

**Question:** Can I rely on the ratings and ra ing systems many magazines use to evaluate colleges?

**Answer:** A number of magazines and Int net sites publish "top 100" style lists of colleges. Other information source collect "best of" information on things like dining hall food, social atmosp ere, and other areas of interest to prospective students and publish their fin gs. Rankings may be reasonable ways to select a restaurant or retail store, t they are lousy ways of selecting your future college. The news and other blications that rank colleges had made their own news of late when a num r of college admitted to or were exposed for falsifying or exaggerating s istics in order to achieve more favorable ratings.

Rankings feed the anxiety of students a parents and do little to facilitate the college exploration, decision-making d application process—but they certainly do sell magazines. It's possible r a quality institution to have an average or weak school of journalism an or a strong school of journalism to be found in an unranked college. The ly ranking that makes any sense is when a student creates a list of college nd where she or he can compete academically, enjoy the living and social menities, and achieve its educa- tional goals. Popular news magazine and I rnet site rankings cannot do that!

**Question:** A friend told me that I should a ly to a couple of safety schools? What is a safety school?

**Answer:** As students narrow their list o colleges, they often include one or two colleges to which they're almost c tain to be accepted—commonly referred to as safety schools. If you choos o apply to a safety school, make sure it is one you like personally and wou want to attend if you are admit- ted. In other words, don't apply to a safet chool just because it's safe.

**Question:** Are there any specific advant es to applying to in-state versus out-of-state colleges?

**Answer:** Applying as a state resident to a ublic university will qualify the student for in-state tuition rates, a reductio that can be significant both annu- ally and over the length of time it takes yo to earn a degree. Some financial aid can only be obtained if applied to fees a in-state institutions. While public university costs are usually lower than pri te institution costs, nonresidents can expect to pay higher costs. All costs t private institutions (in-state or out-of-state) may be offset, however, by the generosity of the grants and scholarships that are available.

**Question:** I've heard that colleges have a profile of the students they know will enroll if accepted. How will this affect my application?

**Answer:** The common student practice of applying to multiple safety schools is one that is under considerable scrutiny by the colleges that had previously accepted these students, who then opted for another institution. A growing number of colleges have been rejecting or wait-listing applicants whom they suspect have selected them as a safeguard.

Through personal interviews, colleges try to gauge a student's interest in attending and weed out those who are less than enthusiastic. They will accept an eager student with slightly lower academic qualifications over a less interested one with stronger qualifications. You can increase your chances of admission by being sincere and genuine in all of your dealings with the colleges that really interest you.

**Question:** What should be some of my concerns if I'm thinking about a community college and then transferring to a four-year school?

**Answer:** Choosing a community college is not any different than choosing a four-year college or university. If your goal is to transfer after two years, then you have the added responsibility of making certain you take classes that will provide credits that the four-year college will accept. Many community colleges and universities have prearranged these course approvals through articulation agreements, resulting in the development of common course descriptions and academic standards designed specifically to aid the eventual transfer student. If you're considering the transfer option, you should seek the advice of an admission counselor at a four-year institution or the personal advice of a student who has been through the experience. Many colleges have one or more counselors who are specifically assigned to work with transfer applicants.

**Question:** What are the requirements that I must complete in order to play sports at the collegiate level?

**Answer:** The National Collegiate Athletic Association (NCAA) has had eligibility standards in effect for some time. A review of the *NCAA Guide for the College-Bound Student-Athlete* found on the NCAA website will present an overview of various eligibility standards and practices that govern the nearly half million student athletes at the collegiate level in the United States. Included in the guide are eligibility rules, recruitment information and calendars, frequently asked questions (FAQs) by student athletes and other information. Your counselor or coach can assist you in the review of this information. Students and parents with eligibility questions can also contact the NCAA Eligibility Center toll free at 8..-282-1492.

**Question:** I think I'm a talented soccer player playing on an "average" high school team. How can I get the attention of college coaches and possibly win an athletic scholarship?

**Answer:** First, you must realize that the competition for athletic scholarships in any sport is extremely high and the number of scholarships awarded to college student-athletes is minimal when compared to the number of high school students in any given sport. Work with your high school coach in an attempt to identify the collegiate level of competition and some of the colleges where your soccer talents might be appropriate. High school and college coaches participate in networks to share information about prospects, and your coach may be able to connect you with some college coaches. Your coach may also be able to forward videotapes that display your soccer skills. Finally, when you talk with admission counselors or visit colleges, make known your interest in the sport and try to connect personally with the coaches and players of the college team.

Remember also that many of the crimes and improprieties that surfaced during the Varsity Blues Scandal in 2019 were tied to inappropriate admission of students masked as student athlete prospects and expect to see additional scrutiny of these types of applications.

**Question:** What are the advantages of attending a historically black college or university?

**Answer:** Students attending one of the more than one hundred black colleges or universities find an academic and social environment that emphasizes African American history and culture. Further, they often find role models in the faculty, administrators, and upper-class students of color that they will be less likely to find on other campuses. The historically black colleges and universities, or HBCUs as they are often called, have a rich tradition of providing quality educational experiences and presenting an alternative learning and living environment for the African American student. HBCUs also help in creating a student bond or kinship that many suggest is not present at more diverse institutions. A campus visit and interaction with enrolled students is certain to point out many of these unique characteristics.

**Question:** How can I find out about colleges that offer special programs for students with learning or physical ability variables and disabilities?
**Answer:** Discovering whether a college can address specific learning variables or physical disabilities should be one of the questions you pose during the exploration process. Direct these questions to the admission counselors or seek the answers from the student service professionals (e.g., counselors,

career advisors, tutors, therapists) responsible for working directly with students with disabilities. You may also wish to check out the resources of the HEATH Resource Center at the National Youth Transitions Center at George Washington University (https://www.heath.gwu.edu/).

**Question:** Our local newspaper recently ran a series of stories about career school scams. How can I avoid enrolling at a bad school?

**Answer:** Once you have found a career or occupational study program that interests you, evaluate it in two ways. First, check to see if the school is accredited by the Accrediting Commission of Career Schools and Colleges (ACCSC). You can review their list of accredited institutions at http://www.accsc.org/Directory/index.aspx.

Second, ask current students or recent graduates to tell you about their educational experiences. If you get positive responses to these two measures, then it is likely the school is a bona fide institution, one capable of providing you with a quality education. These institutions, unfortunately, have had a reputation of exaggerating their graduation rates and job placement records. Be very sensitive to claims that sound too good to be true and to any pressure that may come from staff members to enroll.

**Question:** Are national student award and recognition programs highly regarded by college admission officers?

**Answer:** If you compete and are successful in academic competitions, such as the Regeneron Science Talent Search, Coca Cola Scholars Foundation or the Dupont Challenge, these honors are certain to catch the eye of the admission officer assigned to read your application. The critical element in each of these and similar recognition programs is that real academic and scholarship competition is involved. Some recognition programs are nothing more than individual students submitting academic and extracurricular data for inclusion in a registry or publication. This type of "who's who" recognition carries virtually little or no weight in the admission process. To add insult, you'll also be pestered endlessly to buy a copy of the directory containing your name.

## STUDENT EXER ISE 16.1

### Examining the Admission Competiti 1

One of the best indicators of whether you v ll be admitted to a college is how you stack up against the students that instit ion typically admits. Similar academic qualifications and personal experie es will be viewed positively and often result in admission. This informatio s contained in a first year profile that is published in college guidebooks an iewbooks and sometimes posted on the college website. Students can also e mine the range of admission test scores of the most recently admitted first ar class. Counselors and admission officers can also provide information r this exercise.

College _____
Percentage of applicants that are admitted        _____
Percentage of admitted students that enrol        _____

Senior class standing
Percentage in upper 1/10th of class _____        _____
Percentage in upper 1/4 of class _____        _____
Percentage in upper 1/2 of class _____        _____

Admission test scores
Range of ACT composite scores _____        _____
Range of SAT verbal scores _____        _____
Range of SAT math scores _____        _____
Range of SAT writing scores _____        _____

Admission competition level
____ Highly selective ____ Moderately s ctive ____ Not selective

List below any information you have re ived from students, teachers, or your counselor regarding the academic co petitiveness of the college.

_____        _____
_____        _____
_____        _____
_____        _____

Repeat this exercise for each of the c leges where you are considering applying.

## STUDENT EXERCISE 16.2

### Ranking the Most Important College Characteristics

Review your responses to Student Exercise 5.1, College and University Characteristics: Exploring Your Personal Preferences. List up to ten characteristics (e.g., academic reputation, availability of major, college costs, etc.) below that you feel are the most important in your personal college search. As you review college guides and websites, meet with college admission officers, and visit campuses, examine these characteristics carefully as you evaluate each institution. For this exercise, insert the names of three colleges that you're seriously considering and study the extent to which each institution possesses the characteristics you deem important.

Record your evaluation according to the following scale:

+     Strong presence of the characteristic
O     Modest or limited presence of the characteristic
–     Absence of the characteristic

| College Selection Characteristics | College #1 | College#2 | College #3 |
|---|---|---|---|
| 1. | | | |
| 2. | | | |
| 3. | | | |
| 4. | | | |
| 5. | | | |
| 6. | | | |
| 7. | | | |
| 8. | | | |
| 9. | | | |
| 10. | | | |

## STUDENT EXERCISE 16.3

### The Final Review: Creating Your Application List

Insert below the names of the colleges (in any order) that you continue to consider. To the right, offer an appraisal as to whether the college is a "safe," "probable" or "reach" school. A safe school is one that has a history of admitting students with your type of academic and personal credentials. Probable mean competition will be greater, but your application will be competitive. A reach school suggests that your qualifications are more borderline and the competition for admission is greater. Don create a list made up entirely of reach schools. Your counselor can help you with this appraisal. Finally, list three characteristics (e.g., strong journal m school, friendly atmosphere, affordable, etc.) that have impressed you about the college. These characteristics will be influential in the decisions you are about to make.

College:_____   _Safe___Probable___Reach___
Characteristics that have impressed me during the search process:

    1. _____     _____
    2. _____     _____
    3. _____     _____


College:_____   _Safe___Probable___Reach___
Characteristics that have impressed me during the search process:

    1. _____     _____
    2. _____     _____
    3. _____     _____


College:_____   _Safe___Probable___Reach___
Characteristics that have impressed me during the search process:

    1. _____     _____
    2. _____     _____
    3. _____     _____


College:_____   _Safe___Probable___Reach___
Characteristics that have impressed me during the search process:

    1. _____     _____

2. _____
3. _____


College:_____Safe___Probable___Reach___
Characteristics that have impressed me during the search process:

  1. _____
  2. _____
  3. _____


College:_____Safe___Probable___Reach___
Characteristics that have impressed me during the search process:

  1. _____
  2. _____
  3. _____


College:_____Safe___Probable___Reach___
Characteristics that have impressed me during the search process:

  1. _____
  2. _____
  3. _____

## STUDENT EXEI ISE 16.4

## Application List: Colleges Where You Will Submit Applications

Once you have completed this exercise, re ew the list and the characteristics you have identified for each college. Nex ank the colleges (1 through?) in the order of personal preference. After yc have given full consideration to college costs and the availability of stude t financial aid, you may need to review your ranking.

1. _____       _____
2. _____       _____
3. _____       _____
4. _____       _____
5. _____       _____
6. _____       _____
7. _____       _____
8. _____       _____
9. _____       _____
10. _____       _____

## Chapter 17

# The College Application
## *Making It Work for You*

It's application time. On your desk are a number of envelopes containing application forms, financial aid forms, instruction sheets, and related materials. You may also have accessed the online applications of a number of colleges that want you to submit them electronically. At first glance, the shear enormity of application materials may appear intimidating.

Like all other aspects of the school to college transition, the application phase can produce some anxious, confusing, and stressful times. Coming at the beginning of the senior year, it competes with your efforts to sustain or accelerate your academic efforts and enjoy an extracurricular and social life. You can maintain control by doing the following:

1. Gather all of the forms, instruction sheets, and support materials that are needed to apply for admission and financial aid to the colleges that you are interested in attending. Have everything that you need before you embark on the application submission journey.

2. If the college will accept your application via Common App, Coalition Application, or the Common Black College Application, visit their website at your first convenience to see how they function. A positive feature of these instruments is that students can complete one application and submit it to multiple colleges.

   The Common Application or Common App (https://www.commonapp.org) is accepted by more than 900 colleges and universities. It offers a supplemental section that is used by some colleges to obtain an admission essay. Also available are the Coalition Application (https://www.coalitionforcollegeaccess.org), used by more than 150 institutions, and the Common Black College Application (https://www.commonblackcollegeapp.com), which targets 60 historically Black colleges and universities. Information is avai ole at each site regarding how to use their electronic application.

3. Review all of the applications and cr te a checklist of what needs to be done, who does it, and when it needs o be completed. Determine if the college has an application on its we ite that you can complete online and transmit electronically or print a l send by regular mail.

  Note: If you are applying to a colleg inder an early action, early decision, or restricted early decision pla , the application timetable will be accelerated. Check the college vie ook, website, or with an admission counselor to determine the de line dates for these special plans.

4. Complete the form(s):
   • Read the entire application before mpleting any of the sections.
   • Make copies of the forms and use e copies as worksheets.
   • Follow each direction exactly and ovide all of the information that is requested. Don't feel compelled r forced to fill in every space on the form. Answer the questions tha are relevant to your application.
   • Provide accurate and concise answ s.
   • Prepare a neat application, typing or printing your responses. Edit your responses.

5. Make certain that the required n terials accompany the application, including
   • Essays—Review the essay topics id instructions and devote sufficient time to produce your best wo .
   • Academic records and transcript —Colleges will want copies of your official academic record and anscript to support your application. Direct this request through y ir school counselor, registrar, or records officer.
   • Recommendations—A couple of n-depth recommendations from people who know you and your al ities and achievements are better than many from those who have a sual familiarity. If a college asks for a specific number or designates le specific recommendation writers, be certain to honor its request. rovide guidelines and timetables to these individuals and don't wait til the last minute to request your recommendations.
   • Test scores—If required, schedule ur SAT, ACT, and related testing sessions to allow time (normally si weeks) for score reports to get to the college for proper consideratio
   • Interview—If the college require a personal interview, it is your responsibility to see that it fits inte he admission timetable.
   • Other materials—The college appl ition lists the information needed to evaluate your application. Don send extraneous materials (e.g.,

videos, term papers, newspaper clips, etc.). Most likely, they won't be reviewed.

6. Know the deadline dates and send your applications to the college(s) on time. Procrastination will be your greatest enemy at this stage of the college admission process. Develop an application submission checklist and timetable and stick to them. Should questions arise, consult with your counselor or the college admission/financial aid officers.

## FREQUENTLY ASKED QUESTIONS

**Question:** Is it possible that I could "lose points" with an admission officer because of the appearance of my application?

**Answer:** An application that is messy or difficult to read will certainly detract from the impression you wish to make. If you and another candidate are competing for a spot in the first year class and all other aspects of your application are reasonably equal, the scales might be tipped in favor of the more attractive application. Don't take that chance!

**Question:** What is the Common Application and how may it be used?

**Answer:** The Common Application or Common App is a single college application that is accepted at more than 900 member colleges across the nation. Using the Common Application simplifies the process and reduces the time required because the same information (including essays) can be directed to multiple colleges. Governed by a board comprised of admission officers and secondary school counselors, Common App seeks to promote access, equity and integrity in the school to college transition. The Common App online form and a host of student exploration tools is posted at https://www.commonapp.org/. Your school counselor can answer any questions using this popular tool.

**Question:** How many applications for admission should I submit?

**Answer:** Unless you are very confident in your abilities and your study of the various colleges, filing just one application can be somewhat risky. Most students file multiple applications so that they can increase their exposure to include both safety (you stand a strong chance of being admitted) and reach (you stand a moderate to slim chance of being admitted) schools. The number of applications is not as important as the quality of the exploration and decision making that preceded them.

**Question:** What are the most common mistakes that high school students make in preparing and filing their college applications?

**Answer:** Many students err at the very be[g]inning by failing to read the entire application package before starting to co[m]plete it. Admission officers also cite incompleteness, sloppiness (when usi[ng] print applications), and missing deadlines as common mistakes made by th[e] applicants. With the exception of situations involving an essay or interview[,] he application is all that the college has to evaluate your candidacy, and [y]ou should take considerable care that your application is the best "you" tha[t y]ou can present.

**Question:** I'm considering sending off [mo]re than five admission applications. What am I looking at in application [fe]es?
**Answer:** The range of college applicatio[n] fees is extensive. A recent U.S. News survey reported an average cost p[er] application of $44, including a growing number with fees of $100 and [m]ore. The bottom line is that fil[ing] applications to multiple colleges can [b]e an expensive proposition and students should be on the lookout for fee [w]aivers wherever they may exist. The Common Application posts a fee wa[iv]er form on its website for those member schools offering this provision.

**Question:** I'm considering a college that r[eq]uests that I interview with a representative of the institution. What is the [pu]rpose of this interview?
**Answer:** Colleges request interviews for [a] couple of reasons. Some interviews are part of the evaluation process, a[nd] the interviewer (staff or alumni representative) will prepare a report that w[ill] become part of your application file. Other interviews are informational a[nd] give you an opportunity to ask questions in a private and personal setting. [Y]ou will need to ask the admission officer how the interview will be used. V[Wh]atever the purpose, the key to a successful interview is to be yourself and [be] prepared with questions that are important to your application and eventua[l] enrollment. Not all colleges use the interview in an evaluative sense. They [us]e it to meet you and answer your questions on a more personal level.

**Question:** The colleges I'm interested in [ha]ve all requested personal recommendations. How will they be used?
**Answer:** College recommendations that a[re] prepared by teachers, counselors, or others represent an important aspect [of] the admission decision process for colleges requesting them. Admission [co]unselors read recommendations to gain insight into qualities that are not [ob]vious from objective measures, such as your grade point average or admis[sion] test scores. Recommendations reveal personality, motivations for learni[ng], and philosophy. They give an admission officer a mental snapshot of w[ho] you are. Although it is not the most important item in your application, [a] favorable recommendation is a welcome addition. Submit the number r[eq]uested or recommended on the application. Don't overkill with too many[.]

**Question:** Who should I get to write my college recommendation letters?
**Answer:** First and foremost, follow the instructions on the college application regarding any recommendation letters the college requires. One or two in-depth recommendations from people (e.g., counselor, teachers, and coaches) who know you and your abilities and achievements are better than a handful from those who have a casual familiarity. When approaching your counselor or teachers, provide guidelines and timetables they can follow in getting the recommendations to the colleges. Don't wait to the last minute to ask for their assistance.

**Question:** Last year a student in my high school sent a videotape of one of her drama performances along with her college application? Does this help?
**Answer:** College admission officers, charged with the evaluation of hundreds, sometimes thousands of admission applications, do not have the time to view student videos, and they generally discourage students from submitting such items. However, there are exceptions. Many schools of art, music, and performing arts require students to provide samples of their work and experiences, often in the form of a portfolio, tape, or video. Coaches, too, often like to see videos or films of athletic performances. Read the application materials carefully to determine the policies at each institution.

## STUDENT EXERCISE 17.1

### The College Admission Application Checklist

As you move through the final stages of the admission application process, it is important to organize the various tasks according to a timetable that keeps you in total control of the process. The following checklist will keep you on schedule throughout the application submission period. Ask your counselor to review the checklist to make sure that you have identified all of the tasks that you must complete and you have recorded the correct deadlines. Note: If you are filing under any early decision or early action plan, adjust all completion dates according to the particular plan.

Many colleges permit students to complete admission applications online. Often the submission process is controlled electronically and applicants are guided step by step through the entire process. It is wise to print out a copy of all electronically submitted applications or your admission records and as proof of your submission.

College or University: _____

| Application task | Date Required | Date Completed |
|---|---|---|
| 1. Reviewed college application form or the Common Application and filing requirements. | _____ | _____ |
| 2. Requested transcript be forwarded to college by high school guidance office or registrar. | _____ | _____ |
| 3. Requested letter of recommendation be prepared and forwarded to college by the following individuals: | | |
| _____ | _____ | _____ |
| _____ | _____ | _____ |
| _____ | _____ | _____ |
| 4. Requested test scores be forwarded to college. | _____ | _____ |
| 5. Completed essay (if required). | _____ | _____ |
| 6. Scheduled interview (if required or recommended). | _____ | _____ |

7. Other, specify below:

     _____   _____   _____
     _____   _____   _____
     _____   _____   _____

8. Completed all application      _____   _____
   requirements.

Note: Make additional copies of this form for each college application.

*Chapter 18*

# Understanding College Costs

Paying the college bills has become an expensive proposition for the American student and his or her family. Like most items that we purchase in America, college costs have risen consistently. Over the past two decades, these costs outpaced inflation, and the same is expected to occur for the foreseeable future.

During recent times greater attention has been given by the education community to contain costs and be more transparent in helping the public understand the impact of student debt on everything from the borrowers to the U.S. economy. New Jersey, for example, has enacted legislation requiring all public and private colleges to keep student informed annually about college costs, loan options and the debt they are incurring. In addition to cost containment practices, individual institutions are attempting to offer more gift aid to students in need.

Any attempt to fully understand the world of college costs and financial aid will require students and parents master a vocabulary of words, terms and acronyms that will be required to navigate this part of the college admission process. Routine words like tuition, scholarship and loan get more complicated when the explorer comes across terms like merit aid, need-blind admission and award letter. Throw in a few acronyms like FAFSA (Free Application for Federal Student Aid), SAR (Student Aid Report) and EFC (Expected Family Contribution) and explorers may require help. While a number of these terms will be defined in the following passages, students and families may wish to visit a comprehensive glossary that College Board has posted at https://bigfuture.collegeboard.org/pay-for-college/financial-aid-101/financial-aid-glossary-learnthe-lingo#. The annual College Board college cost report which surveys college costs on an annual basis can be found nearby at https://research.collegeboard.org/trends/college-pricing/. At the same time, more and more students are competing for the billions of dollars in financial assistance made available by government, institutions, and private sources to postsecondary students each year.

Studies by the U.S. Department of Education report that as many as 8 to 10% college students will use some form financial aid before they graduate. All of these conditions warrant students' and their families' understanding just what they are paying for and exercising control when options exist. College costs fall into two categories: fixed and controllable.

## FIXED COSTS

These costs are the same for all students. They include tuition, room and board, and student fees.

Tuition is the cost of your education and is set by the institution or by the governing authority overseeing the institution or system of higher education. Room and board costs are fixed if the student is required to live on campus, a situation that is often the case for first-year students. Student fees range from the activities fee (providing access to athletic and cultural events) to laboratory and library fees.

Note: A number of colleges have experimented with fixed or limited-increase tuition plans. In these situations, students entering college at a particular point know the cost of tuition and the adjustments they can expect to see during their total enrollment period.

## CONTROLLABLE COSTS

These are the costs for which the student can exercise some degree of spending authority. They include books, materials, and fees (i.e., Internet access, etc.), personal expenses, transportation, and room and board (off campus). Book costs can be controlled somewhat by the acquisition of used books and either purchasing or renting textbooks online. Personal expenses such as entertainment, clothing, and sundries are influenced by preference, need, and consumption rates. Think about the items (e.g., shampoo, snacks, stamps, etc.) you need and consume today. When you get to college, the cost of these things will come out of your personal expenses budget.

Transportation costs, which vary by the distance between the student's home and the campus, are affected by the method of transportation that one uses to get back and forth and how often the student travels. Room and board costs can be controlled when the student resides off campus or has variable campus meal plans available.

Another controllable cost factor is the ability of the student to complete his or her studies in four years. The time it takes to attain a degree has been steadily creeping upward and this means additional costs for the fifth or sixth year. Students who transfer from one college to another are sometimes unable to complete their studies in four years.

College is expensive and often explorers are interested in calculating the "return on investment," or ROI, of college degree attainment. Given the range of expenses and the limited ability that students have to exercise control, it is important that costs, aid opportunities, and options be fully examined and understood. Cost should never be used as the factor or criterion that solely guides exploration, and no college should ever be excluded from consideration due to cost until the student knows what type of financial assistance package might be assembled by the financial aid office.

Understanding college costs is only half of the information that students and their families must possess. You must also understand the college student financial aid system and the various forms of assistance that are available. It is information you won't regret researching.

## FREQUENTLY ASKED QUESTIONS

**Question:** Is it possible to get a sense of what the actual costs of enrolling at a particular college will be during the exploration process?
**Answer:** Colleges that participate in the federal student aid programs are required to have a net-price calculator available on their websites. Each calculator helps the student and parents understand better, through specific calculation, the total cost at the college or university. It can be found on either the "Admission" or "Financial Aid" link of the school's website.

**Question:** Are college costs in any way controllable or does everyone pay the same amount?
**Answer:** College costs can be controlled to a limited extent. While tuition, fees, and room and board, for the most part, are the same for all students, you might be able to modify your living arrangements or meal plan to control costs somewhat. Many of the things you pay for are based on frequency or consumption. These include books where you can save by purchasing used textbooks and personal expenses such as movies, long-distance telephone calls, snacks, dry cleaning, stamps, and related items.

Transportation costs from college to home can also be controlled by the frequency of the travel and the mode of transportation used. If you are given the option or opportunity to live off campus and this is something you wish to do, you will find housing costs vary considerably in each college community.

**Question:** I need to go to a college my family and I can afford. How strongly should cost influence my decision?

**Answer:** Cost should be a consideration ...ly after you look at whether the college is the right place for you academi...lly and socially. In other words, will the institution present you with acade...ic challenges you can live up to? Next, will you enjoy the social setting a... lifestyle offered by the college and the community? The cost of college ...ll play heavily on your eventual decision, but don't make it the only or fi... ingredient in your examination. Remember, many financial aid programs ...e available to help you meet college expenses. Try to get an idea of the a... you might be eligible for as you weigh the financial factor in your selectio... process.

**Question:** Have colleges ever been kn...wn to cut their costs or offer discounts?

**Answer:** Unlike commercial establishme..., colleges do not have sales and bargain days. This, however, does not m...an that everyone pays the same. Institutions have been diligent in their qu...to contain costs (i.e., fixed rates for the full period of enrollment, campu...ased work-study programs) and find new sources of aid. The result is tha...illions of dollars in institutional aid is awarded each year by the colleges th...nselves. Such aid is far more limited at public institutions where costs can...e substantially lower. Since each institution is spending its own resources, t...criteria for getting this assistance will vary, but demonstrated need is a com...on criterion.

**Question:** Is it true that college student e...loyment is on the rise?

**Answer:** The National Center for Educa...n Statistics (NCES) surveys are indicating the employment by full-time u...ergraduate students is on the rise as more than half those enrolled are perf...ming some compensation-driven work. Being employed does contribute to...udent study and living costs, but also presents challenges for academic per...rmance and lengthens the enrollment period beyond that traditionally requ...ed for degree attainment.

## STUDENT EXERCISE 18.1

### Determining College Costs: A Personal Budgeting Process

Use the spaces below to identify the costs associated with those colleges that you are interested in attending. Accurate college tuition, room and board, and related costs can be found in the literature distributed by each institution. Since costs fluctuate greatly from year to year, make certain that you have current figures.

| Expenses | College | College | College |
|---|---|---|---|
| Tuition and fees | _____ | _____ | _____ |
| Room and board | _____ | _____ | _____ |
| Books, supplies, materials, etc. | _____ | _____ | _____ |
| Living expenses | _____ | _____ | _____ |
| Transportation | _____ | _____ | _____ |
| Other expenses, specify: | | | |
| _____ | _____ | _____ | _____ |
| _____ | _____ | | |
| _____ | _____ | | |
| Total college budget | _____ | _____ | _____ |

*Chapter 19*

# Types and Sources of
# Student Financial Aid

Education after high school is a major investment for students and families and financing higher education today has become a major challenge. Part of the challenge is to learn how the financial aid system works and the degree to which the various forms of student financial aid will offset the rising costs.

The financial aid system in American higher education operates according to the following basic principle: Students and their families contribute to the cost of college to the extent or level they are able. The difference between their ability to contribute and the cost of going to college is referred to as "need." Consider the following formula:

**Cost of college – student/family contribution = financial aid eligibility**

Since much of the student assistance in this nation comes from federal sources, guidelines established by the Congress and administered by the U.S. Department of Education provide the structure for both government-driven and other student financial aid programs and policies. To qualify for federal assistance and for much of the aid offered by related sources, students must demonstrate need.

Even though college costs may vary, the family contribution remains constant. The student's financial aid eligibility increases as the cost increases, one important reason that students should not exclude colleges from consideration simply on the basis of cost.

There are three basic types of federal student financial aid:

Grants and gift aid—Grants are gift aid and do not have to be repaid. The amount of the federal grant will vary from year to year, dependent on the funds that have been appropriated for the grant programs.

Work-study—Work-study is student assistance in the form of employment at your college. This part-time employment provides you an opportunity to earn money (at least at current federal minimum wage levels) to offset the cost of your schooling.

Student loans—Loans enable students and parents to borrow funds to meet educational costs. These loans must be repaid with interest.

To ask questions, order free publications, and learn more about the federal student aid programs, call 1–800–4FED-AID (1–800–433–3243). TTY 1–800–730–8913. You can also contact the Department of Education at http://studentaid.ed.gov/contact#email-us.

Beyond the federal aid programs, students will find financial aid available from state governments, private sources, and from the colleges themselves. State governments typically require demonstrated need and residency, but may have other eligibility criteria as well.

Private scholarship programs are offered by corporations, public service, and fraternal organizations, foundations, labor unions, and other philanthropic groups. These are both merit- and need-based. Once you have narrowed the list of colleges to a reasonable number, inquire as to the availability of scholarships and grants from those institutions. Colleges differ in their ability to meet the needs of their students. High-cost colleges typically put together larger student aid packages, often combining grants, work-study, and loans.

Students and families need to be aware of the terms under which scholarships are offered and any requirements (e.g., maintenance of a specific grade point average) for its continuance. Because of the perception that only the neediest families qualify for assistance, many students do not even apply for assistance. All families should examine the various sources of aid and determine the extent to which they can and should participate.

No search of scholarships, however, would be complete without examining local sources available to graduates of a particular high school or residents of a specific community. Some larger businesses and companies have scholarships for the children of their employees. School counselors can provide general information about local sources and types of financial assistance. College financial aid officers are experts in the federal, state, and institution programs and can provide details about the lending opportunities and terms offered at commercial banks.

## ASKING THE RIGHT FINANCIAL AID QUESTIONS

If enrolling at a particular college is going to depend on securing a workable financial aid package, the student is going to have to ask a number of questions, save and compare the answers, and factor the findings into the application and enrollment decision. The following questions should be considered and each student may have others to add:

1. How much need-based and merit-based aid is available from the college?
2. How does one get the eligibility information, forms and deadlines for this aid?
3. What exact costs will the financial aid office use in determining eligibility for assistance?
4. Are there any hidden costs (computer and lab fees, special events participation, etc.) that are dependent on consumption and use?
5. Does the financial aid package extend beyond the initial year?
6. Will any merit-based aid received have academic requirements that must be met to continue receiving it?
7. How is aid from external sources factored into the student's overall need calculation?
8. How much college loan indebtedness are students accumulating at the college or university?
9. What is the college doing to ensure that students graduate debt-free?
10. What percentage of enrolled students graduate in four, five or more years?
11. Does the college have any payment options or plans that might ease the impact of the college bills?

## FREQUENTLY ASKED QUESTIONS

**Question:** Help me to understand the purpose of financial aid. Isn't it designed to help students with considerable need pay for college?
**Answer:** Financial aid comes in multiple forms directed at students in varied situations. You are correct in assuming that a considerable amount of financial aid is targeted at students who wouldn't be able to go to college without this help. But that number has risen steadily as college costs have increased. Today, two-thirds or more of the students on many campuses are receiving some form of financial aid. Aid based on financial circumstances is referred to as need-based aid. Aid that is awarded on the basis of individual talent or personal accomplishment is known as merit-based aid.

Merit-based aid is typically associated with the achievements the college-bound student has earned or for the special talents they possess. Often merit assistance does not take need into account and can be awarded to any student meeting the criteria. In other instances, financial aid may be awarded on the basis of both need and merit. Since some merit-based awards are competitive, you will need to conduct thorough study of these sources to determine eligibility and file the necess y applications.

**Question:** Exactly what is the FAFSA an vho should be using it?
**Answer:** FAFSA is short for the Free Ap lication for Federal Student Aid, an application used by virtually all fou and two-year colleges and universities and other postsecondary institu ons awarding federal, state and institution-sponsored student aid. For gen al information about the federal student aid programs, assistance in compl ing the FAFSA, and information about FAFSA on the Web, call the Feder Student Aid Information Center (FSAIC) at the following toll-free number -800-433-3243.

**Question:** Student borrowing, loans, an the huge debt that is generated has been getting a lot of attention in the f ancial news lately. How do these loans work?
**Answer:** Student loans are helping many llege students earn their degrees today. A student, parent, or guardian ma take out a load that the federal government subsidizes or guarantees, one hat must be repaid with interest, which is tax deductible. The rising cost of college and university education in the United States, along with career an educational interruptions brought on by the coronavirus pandemic, have ma borrowing and the record levels of student and young adult debt a major s ietal concern.

**Question:** How much are students conce ed about college costs and their student budgets?
**Answer:** When first year college stude around the nation were asked recently about college costs and bearing th e expenses on a recent American College Freshman survey, 81% indicate that cost and the availability of financial aid was a factor in determining here they applied and eventually enrolled. In addition, 61% stated they had orked during high school to help pay for college, a factor that most believe y would have to continue during their college enrollment. Two-thirds (64% f freshmen students have lingering concerns about their college financing

**Question:** How serious is the student de problem brought on by college students borrowing to pay their college co s?
**Answer:** As more students and families ar becoming dependent on financial assistance, many institutions are attemptin to contain costs and expand support to students. As a result, the number o tudents borrowing to meet rising college costs and the amount they are bor wing is increasing. Students and parents loathe the thought of limiting colle choices, but if the eventual decision would leave the student or family wi a mountain of debt, some limits may be in order.

Recent government and media reports have called public attention to growing concern that one in four Americans is affected in some manner by student debt. For some time, students and families have been forced to borrow to make up for less than adequate financial aid packages and the end result has been an enormous growth in the debt of the U.S. young adult population that lingers for many, many years.

**Question:** I'm confused about just who makes financial aid available to students. Can you help me?

**Answer:** College student financial aid comes from basically three sources: government (federal and state), institutions, and the private sector. Federal and state aid is available in the form of grants, work-study programs, and scholarships, each having different need and eligibility requirements. Institutional aid represents those dollars that a particular college has to disperse to aid students it is hoping to enroll. Finally, a considerable amount of assistance is made available by corporations, foundations, philanthropic groups, and service organizations to students meeting their award criteria. While much of the aid from the latter group is awarded through national competition, some local sources restrict their aid to students from a given high school, residents of a particular community, or children of their employees.

Your school counselor, librarian, and the financial aid officer at the college you're considering will be a valuable source of information about these programs. If you are searching for scholarships, you should also check out www.finaid.com which has been tracking scholarships for some time and has an extensive database.

**Question:** The college I want to attend is offering me less in my financial aid package than another college. Is there any way for me to use that offer to bargain with my first choice?

**Answer:** At the risk of making the process sound like purchasing a used car, the current college admission and financial aid climate offers the talented student more opportunity for negotiation than he or she might believe. There is nothing wrong with letting your first-choice college know about the financial aid package being offered by another institution. Private colleges, for example, have some latitude in shaping their aid packages, and, in some instances, you may see an adjustment to your original offer. Public colleges will not have the same flexibility.

Don't ever present your situation as a "match it or I'm outta here" kind of ultimatum. There are many qualified individuals seeking admission who are just as deserving and in need of the college's aid as you.

**Question:** An admission officer at a private college told me to look beyond costs to possible financial aid when comparing public and private colleges. What did she mean?

**Answer:** What the admission officer was saying was that on the surface private colleges often seem twice, sometimes three or four times, as expensive as public colleges. But private institutions have the ability to put together more flexible and usually larger financial aid packages for the students they hope will enroll. It's important not to remove any college from consideration solely on the basis of cost.

**Question:** What does "need-blind" admission mean?

**Answer:** The term "need-blind" means that the college's admission decision is not based in any way on a person's financial need and that any financial aid decisions are made independently, usually in a different office of the college. A number of colleges are "need conscious," rather than need-blind, which means they will examine a student's financial status in making admission decisions. If his or her need is too great, and the college cannot offer a financial aid package to cover that amount of need, the student may be denied admission. Fortunately for you, a majority of colleges employ a need-blind policy, and, at these schools, your financial status will not influence your chances for admission. If you have a concern, ask the admission office to explain the manner in which decisions are made at their institution.

**Question:** What is the difference between a scholarship and a grant?

**Answer:** In the language of a financial aid officer, a scholarship and a grant are basically the same thing. Both are "gift" aid, meaning they do not need to be paid back. Some forms of gift aid, however, may require that you meet certain requirements like maintaining a certain grade point average or majoring in a particular field. Make sure you understand any terms or restrictions that are associated with any assistance you receive before you accept the aid.

**Question:** What are work-study programs and how can I find out about them from the colleges I'm applying to?

**Answer:** Work-study is a form of need-based financial aid where a student may earn money by working on campus or with an approved off-campus employer. Work-study is usually packaged with grants, scholarships, and loans to reduce costs and make the college experience more affordable. Students considering any type of employment need to be sensitive to balancing study and work. Otherwise, the work experience can have a negative effect on classroom performance and can easily interrupt one's academic program. The financial aid office at the college will have information about work-study opportunities and their eligibility requirements.

**Question:** When a college offers me a financial aid package, is it good for all four years or is my situation evaluated each year?

**Answer:** Some of the scholarships you may be offered will be good for the entire four years. Some may not. Be certain that you understand the duration of the gift and the conditions (e.g., maintaining a certain grade point average) under which you accept it. The Pell Grant program, the largest federal student assistance program, is based on need and your situation will be evaluated each year to determine your eligibility. Be leery of institutions that "front load" your assistance to get you to enroll and then leave you to your own devices, such as taking out student loans, to pay for the remaining years.

**Question:** I've seen the term "family contribution" in several books about financial aid. What does it mean?

**Answer:** You may be referring to the "expected family contribution" or EFC. This is the amount, determined by a congressional formula, that a student's family is expected to contribute toward the cost of attending college. It is factored into all federal student assistance awards. The EFC is printed on the front of the Student Aid Report (SAR) that you will receive following the processing of the Free Application for Federal Student Aid (FAFSA). This information is also forwarded to colleges.

**Question:** Are competitive scholarships worth pursuing?

**Answer:** When your abilities, achievements, and interests fall in line with a particular scholarship program and the scholarship looks like it was meant for you, go after it with vigor and enthusiasm. Unfortunately, this will not always be the case. If you knew the number of students competing for some scholarship programs, you might consider buying a lottery ticket instead. If the scholarship requires completion of a tedious application or completion of some other requirement (e.g., essay), you may wish to consider the yield versus the effort you must expend. When you research scholarships, try to determine the number of scholarships awarded in comparison to the number of applicants. You will soon recognize that some scholarships are next to impossible to get. Don't forget the scholarships awarded right in your high school and community. They may not be large dollar awards, but they won't attract thousands of applicants either.

**Question:** What does loan forgiveness mean?

**Answer:** A number of government agencies at various levels have pitched in to help college graduates pay off the debt from their student loans. These programs are often created to attract graduates to high need areas for certain occupations (e.g., health workers in distant rural areas). The longer the individual works in the setting, the greater the amount of loan forgiveness. Many business and corporate employers also have programs like this. These are designed as an employee benefit to rev ırd employees for their work and service in the hopes of retaining a solid  am of efficient, productive, and debt-free workers.

## STUDENT EXERCISE 19.1

### Examining the Availability of Financial Aid

Take time to talk with your counselor and the admission and financial aid representatives of the college(s) you are interested in attending. Spend some time reviewing the financial aid guidebooks and computer disks in your guidance office or library. From those discussions and your research, create a list of scholarships, grants, work-study programs, and loans. In the space below, make a list of financial aid opportunities for which you wish to get applications and eligibility criteria.

Source                    Type of Assistance        Comments
Federal/National

_____

_____

_____

_____

State

_____

_____

_____

_____

Local

_____

_____

_____

_____

Institution

_____

_____

_____

_____

Private

_____

_____

_____

_____

*Chapter 20*

# Making Financial Aid
# Forms Work for You

If completing the collection of college admission forms you've assembled wasn't enough, you'll soon discover that financial aid application forms will require equal time and attention. Unless you're one of the third of college students not receiving some form of financial assistance, you will need to file original forms and update or refile them each year you wish to remain an aid recipient.

The process begins by making certain that you have the right forms. Some will be available from your high school guidance office. Others will come directly from the college or from the agency, firm, or organization making the award. Other forms, like loan applications, must be obtained from the banks or lending institutions. It's a good idea to ask for financial aid forms at the time you are gathering your admission applications.

Once assembled, it is always a good idea to review all of the forms to determine what information you will need to respond to the questions. Since financial aid is often based on need, many of the questions will address family financial matters. Your parents need to be involved in their completion and must attest to their accuracy.

To be considered for the federal student aid programs (e.g., Federal Pell Grants and Federal Family Education Loans), a student must complete the Free Application for Federal Student Aid (FAFSA) which was described in earlier chapters. This application collects financial aid and other information used to calculate the Expected Family Contribution (EFC) that ultimately determines the student's eligibility for aid. Visit https://studentaid.gov/aid-estimator/ to learn more.

Students and parents needing help with either the print or electronic versions of these federal programs and encouraged to call the toll-free federal student aid information number: 1–800–4FEDAID (1–800–433-3243).

In a few weeks following the submissi⋯ ⋯ of the FAFSA, you'll receive a Student Aid Report (SAR). The SAR con⋯ ⋯ins the information that you provided on the FAFSA, plus your EFC. Thi⋯ ⋯is the figure that the college will use in determining your eligibility for fe⋯ ⋯al student aid. It is your responsibility to check the SAR and make sure ⋯ ⋯at everything is correct. Also, be certain that your current address is alway⋯ ⋯on file with the U.S. Department of Education.

If you are an applicant for institutional ⋯ ⋯id, you may be required to complete the CSS/Profile or a college-specif⋯ ⋯ financial aid application. These forms will request information beyond th⋯ ⋯on the FAFSA, information that the colleges feel is important in their asses⋯ ⋯ent of need. The CSS/Profile can be accessed at the College Board website: ⋯ ⋯p://student.collegeboard.org/css-financial-aid-profile. Unlike the FAFSA, f⋯ ⋯ng the CSS/Profile is not free and the student should check with choice coll⋯ ⋯es to make certain it is required.

In addition to the FAFSA, CSS/Profil⋯ ⋯ and college-specific forms, you will need a number of other items when ⋯ ⋯ou and your parents sit down to complete this important task. These inclu⋯ ⋯ (1) your most recent tax return, (2) your parents' most recent tax return, ⋯ ⋯d (3) other records such as W-2 forms, bank statements, business/farm rec⋯ ⋯ds, and investment records.

During the process of completing the va⋯ ⋯ous forms, make certain that you answer all of the relevant questions with t⋯ ⋯ most current and accurate information. Sign each form (some require both ⋯ ⋯tudent and parent signatures) and send them off to the appropriate processin⋯ ⋯ agency or office. Be sensitive to deadlines as many scholarships, grants, an⋯ ⋯nstitutional awards have cyclical application periods or award the assistanc⋯ ⋯on a first come, first served basis.

## FREQUENTLY ASKED QUESTIONS

**Question:** It looks like I will have to apply ⋯ ⋯or financial aid. Will I have to file a Free Application for Federal Student A⋯ ⋯ (FAFSA) and CSS/Profile with every college where I will submit an appli⋯ ⋯ation?
**Answer:** Once you file the FAFSA and C⋯ ⋯/Financial Aid Profile, the information they generate will likely meet the ⋯ ⋯eds of the colleges to which you apply. There can be situations, however, ⋯ ⋯hen a college will want you to complete a specific application for aid th⋯ ⋯ it administers. The same is true for independent and private scholarships ⋯ ⋯at are likely to request their own application.

**Question:** What are the most critical d⋯ ⋯es in the financial aid application calendar?

**Answer:** There are at least two sets of dates, and possibly many others that you will need to learn and juggle as you apply for the various forms of financial aid you might be considering. Your best bet is to put together an admission and financial aid calendar that lists all of the tasks you need to perform. This calendar should include at least three columns, one each for the name of the award, the filing deadline, and the date you want to have the application completed.

**Question:** Am I required to complete the Free Application for Federal Student Aid if I'm not eligible for federal government assistance?
**Answer:** The FAFSA is the "rock" upon which most financial aid decisions are built. Whether you feel you are eligible for federal student assistance or not, you should prepare and file a FAFSA as soon after the beginning of January in your senior year as possible. A second form, the CSS/Profile is required by 400 colleges and scholarship programs and requires a $25 fee for one report and $16 for additional submissions. All of this information is then used by the financial aid office in determining your personal financial aid package. File these forms as early as possible and consult with your school counselor if necessary.

**Question:** How can I recognize the rip-off schemes of scholarship search firms?
**Answer:** "If it sounds too good to believe . . . it probably is" is an old adage that has particular relevance here. Services that make outrageous claims like "billions of dollars in financial aid goes unclaimed each year" are worthy of considerable scrutiny before you make payment for services. The best advice for those concerned about fee-charging financial aid services is to exhaust the counseling services of the high school and the college admission and financial aid office before purchasing these services from independent sources.

Many services provide little real help for the fees charged, which can range from $50 to $250 or more for a scholarship search service that you can most likely conduct yourself on the Internet. The Bureau of Consumer Protection and Federal Trade Commission have established an Internet website where you can learn more about the questionable practices of some of these firms. Visit http://www.consumer.ftc.gov/articles/0082-scholarship-and-financial-aid-scams.

## STUDENT EXERCISE 20.1

### Financial Aid Application Checklist

Much like the admission application process, your applications for scholarships, grants, and other forms of financial aid are going to require specific attention. The following checklist will keep you on schedule throughout this period. Your counselor or a financial aid advisor at the colleges you're considering can also provide guidance in the completion of these forms. As family financial information is usually required on these forms, allow sufficient time for your parents to participate.

Whether you submit a paper or electronic application for financial aid, you need to recognize that some forms must be filed with the federal government, state government, or other national entities that help to determine your eligibility for assistance. Make certain you understand these requirements and the order in which they must be completed. Your application for institutional assistance and some private scholarships could be predicated on those requirements already being met.

| Financial Aid Application Task | Date Required | Date Completed |
|---|---|---|
| 1. Completed and submitted FAFSA. | _____ | _____ |
| 2. Completed and submitted CSS/Profile | _____ | _____ |
| 3. Requested federal financial aid report forwarded to college(s). | _____ | _____ |
| 4. Requested CSS/Profile report forwarded to college(s). | _____ | _____ |
| 5. Completed appropriate state financial aid form(s). | _____ | _____ |
| 6. Completed appropriate institution-specific financial aid form(s). | _____ | _____ |
| 7. Completed application(s) for work-study programs. | _____ | _____ |

| Financial Aid Application Task | Date Required | Date Completed |
|---|---|---|
| 8. Completed scholarship application form(s) required by the college. | _____ | _____ |
| 9. Completed application(s) for private scholarships (national and local). | _____ | _____ |
| 10. Other, specify: | _____ | _____ |

_____

_____

_____

_____

*Chapter 21*

# After the Application

## *What Happens Next?*

When the application for admission has been reviewed by a college, one of four actions can result. If you have explored properly and applied to colleges where the students reflect the academic characteristics and personal qualities that you present, there is a strong likelihood that an acceptance letter will find its way to your mailbox.

According to the Higher Education Research Institute, 73% of a recent college first year class said they had been accepted by their first-choice college. That's a good acceptance rate, but one marred by the fact that only 55% of those students had actually enrolled at their most favored college. The disparity between the two percentages can be attributed to a number of things, but most likely because the first-choice offer of admission had to be rejected because the college was too expensive and unable to meet the full financial need of the applicant.

If offered admission to more than one institution, you have the pleasant (and possibly difficult) task of deciding where you will enroll in the fall. If an application is not accepted, there are three other outcomes. Let's look at each.

*Conditional Admission*—A conditional admission means that your admission is dependent upon your meeting some special or additional requirement (e.g., summer study, midyear enrollment). Contact the college admission office directly to make certain you understand the terms of the admission and your time line for meeting these requirements.

*Wait-List*—If you're wait-listed, you have a right to know the wait-list history of the institution. In other words, how many people typically move from the list to general admission? If you can review the wait-list history for a couple of earlier classes, you'll get some sense of your status and whether you should hold out hope of enrollment. If your applications result in a combination of acceptances and wait-list responses, you'll need to consider these variables as the date approaches for responding to your offers of admission.

Again, it is wise to consult with the admission officer(s) and your counselor for interpretation and guidance.

*Application Denied*—Some students who are denied admission take it upon themselves to appeal the decision, especially if they feel that the decision didn't take all of the appropriate factors into account. While certainly a long shot, this avenue is open to you and should be taken if there is any indication that the college acted without full information.

If all of your applications are rejected you should confer immediately with your counselor and map out an alternate course of action. There may be appropriate colleges that are still taking applications, even at this late point in the admission cycle. If you need to strengthen your academic status, you might enroll in a junior or community college or engage in additional preparatory studies and reapply as a transfer applicant.

Many two-year institutions have articulation agreements with four-year colleges and universities where credits are accepted by the senior school and a "seamless" transition occurs whereby the student completes two years at the community college and then continues directly on to a collaborating baccalaureate degree–granting school. Students denied admission should definitely consider this fallback position.

A student receiving acceptance letters should be prepared to inform the one college that he or she wishes to attend of their enrollment decision by May 1, the date viewed by the collegiate community as the universal reply date. The precise language in the NACAC Guide to Ethical Practice in College Admission states that a college will "permit students for fall admission to choose among offers of admission, financial aid, and scholarships until May 1 and will state this deadline explicitly in their offers of admission."

Along with your letter of notification you may be asked to send an admission or housing deposit to confirm your enrollment intentions. Under no circumstances should you declare your intention to enroll at more than one college.

If you're faced with the situation in which you've been accepted to more than one college, you must once again weigh the criteria that you studied in making your application decisions and determine which one of these colleges will present you with the best learning and living situation. When the academic and social scales are even, it may boil down to cost or the financial aid offer, but avoid using these criteria as your primary guide. After letting your new college know that you're accepting their offer of admission, let the others that tendered you an acceptance know of that decision.

Occasionally, a student gets to this point in the admission process and determines he or she can't or doesn't want to go to college immediately. There can be many reasons for this, including "readiness" to do college work or having insufficient funds to go immediately after high school graduation.

Other students simply need to take a break from school before heading off to four more years. Whatever the reason, this student should consider a "gap year" in order to get academic or financial issues under control.

Keep your academic work up throughout the remainder of your senior year and begin making plans to be a college student. Congratulations. The exploration, decision-making, and application journey is now complete. Exciting times await you at the college that you have just selected!

## FREQUENTLY ASKED QUESTIONS

**Question:** I know where I want to apply. What I don't know is where I will enroll if more than one college accepts me. Can you advise?
**Answer:** This second decision may be more difficult than the first. Deciding where to enroll means going back over everything that caused you to consider the college in the first place. If possible, revisit the college, stay overnight, visit a class, eat the food, and live the life of a college student for a day. Concentrate on getting answers to the following three questions. Does it offer the right academic opportunities and promise of success? Will you feel comfortable living on the campus and in the community? Are the college costs, when viewed in light of your family resources and available aid, affordable? Consider the pluses and minuses, and one of the colleges will take center stage. That's where you should enroll.

**Question:** What can I do if all the colleges I applied to reject me?
**Answer:** Don't panic! If you thought your application was misinterpreted in any way or that something was overlooked, then you should contact the college. Write a concise letter strongly stating your position and most colleges will gladly give your application a second look. If pleading your case is not an option, confer with your high school counselor and try to determine if any other colleges have vacancies that are compatible with your academic qualifications and personal characteristics. If you need to strengthen your academic status, you may wish to enroll in a community or junior college or engage in some form of remedial study. After you have enhanced your academic background, you can reapply or submit a transfer application in a year or two.

**Question:** What if more than one college offers me admission and they both want a deposit immediately?
**Answer:** According to the NACAC Guide to Ethical Practice in College Admission, you have the right to wait until May 1 to respond to any admission and/or financial aid offers. Colleges that request such commitment prior to May 1 should still offer you the opportunity to request an extension (in

writing) until May 1. (This right does not apply to early decision candidates.) You can consult the statement at http://www.nacacnet.org/about/Governance/Policies/Documents/SPGP.pdf.

**Question:** How can I improve my chances of admission if I'm placed on a wait-list?

**Answer:** If you are wait-listed at a college where you would really like to enroll, you first need to determine the typical wait-list movement at the institution. Colleges are usually willing to provide a history (some even include it in your wait-list notification) that describes the number of students wait-listed, the number eventually offered admission, and the availability of financial aid and housing for them. Your potential admission is controlled by the number of acceptances the college receives to its regular offers of admission. You may wish to write a note to the admission office indicating your continued interest in the college. Throughout the process, however, study each of your other options carefully so you have a definite course of action to follow should you not be removed from the wait-list.

**Question:** I recently heard a student say that her admission letter stated that her acceptance was "conditional." What does that mean?

**Answer:** By necessity, the admission calendar requires that you submit an application long before you complete high school. In fact, the transcript that accompanies your application will contain grades for approximately half of your senior year, less if you have applied under an early decision or early action plan. The college will expect that your final transcript reflects the same level of academic performance after acceptance as before. Some would go so far as to state that your acceptance is "conditional," meaning that your acceptance can be revoked if you fail to maintain your current level of performance.

**Question:** Once I've been admitted to a college, will the admission office really care about my final high school grades and academic record?

**Answer:** You bet. A serious case of the "senior slump" could have a dramatic effect on your future. The offer of admission is a lot like a contract, a contract with certain contingencies. One such contingency is that you continue your academic performance at a level that justified your acceptance. Why would you want to break stride with a formula that has brought you the reward of college admission? Remember that higher education will make greater demands on you. If you maintain good study habits, you will have an easier time when you begin your college experience.

**Question:** When can I expect the college to ask me and my parents for some money?

**Answer:** When you receive your offer of admission, just about every college will ask you to submit a housing deposit along with the confirmation that you will be attending their institution. These deposits vary from as low as $250 to as high as $1,000 or more, but that amount is eventually deducted from your first year bill. Dorm selection can be tied to the deposit being placed to secure your enrollment and eventual housing location. The remainder of your tuition, room and board, and related costs will be expected closer to the time you register for classes or according to the various payment plans your college might offer.

**Question:** If I elect to take a "gap year," will my acceptance to college be valid when I want to start?

**Answer:** Colleges differ in the manner in which they treat requests for deferred admission. Some will support your decision and keep your offer of admission open. Others may have guidelines for doing this or reject your request and make you reapply. Consult with an admission counselor as soon as you determine a gap year is in your future plans.

## STUDENT EXERCISE 21.1

### From Admission to Enrollment: A Brief Checklist

College decision making has multiple stages. First, you must decide what colleges to examine. Then you need to decide where to submit applications. The final decision often is the most important. Where will you enroll if accepted? Remember the same criteria that you used when determining where to apply should now be repeated in determining where to enroll.

The following yes/no checklist will allow you to reconsider all of the factors involved in the final selection of your college and may prove useful in pointing you in the right direction.

| Enrollment Issues | College A Yes / No | College B Yes / No | College C Yes / No |
|---|---|---|---|
| The college has the courses and/or major I want to study. | _____ | _____ | _____ |
| I am capable of meeting the academic challenges of the college. | _____ | _____ | _____ |
| The college seems like the right place for me to live and learn. | _____ | _____ | _____ |
| The community offers the resources (e.g., church, cultural activities, etc.) I will use and enjoy. | _____ | _____ | _____ |
| The college is affordable. | _____ | _____ | _____ |
| The financial aid package offered meets my expectations. | _____ | _____ | _____ |
| _____ | _____ | _____ | _____ |
| _____ | _____ | _____ | _____ |

# Chapter 22

# Off to College

## *Getting Ready for Your First Year*

The time between graduation in late May or early June and starting college in August or September is going to be packed full of more things that need attention than you could have ever imagined. Along with your offer of admission, or soon after you indicate you wish to enroll, your college of choice will begin sending you information that will facilitate the enrollment process.

This information may come from the admission office, the financial aid office, the housing department, and any number of other points of contact on your future campus. Just open these envelopes as they arrive and do everything the college instructs you to do to become fully enrolled.

The months ahead will require that you perform a series of tasks that prepare you to head off to college when summer ends. If you are going to become a residential student, you will be moving to your new college address, a transition that in no small way is like moving from one home to another. Think about all the things that you will require for your relocation and then take the necessary actions.

For example, do you have a checking account now, one that you're going to simply maintain while away at college or are you going to open an account when you get to school. How about an ATM card for those times when you need to put your hands on some quick cash? Are there any change-of-address notifications (e.g., magazine subscriptions, etc.) that you need to make? Tasks of this nature require some lead time. Give yourself sufficient time.

Will you need to acquire items (e.g., desk lamps, compact refrigerator, etc.) to make your dorm room more comfortable and functional? Do you have all the learning and study resources (e.g., word-processing software, dictionary, thesaurus, etc.) needed to function away from home? Make the identification or acquisition of these items an all-summer activity and don't leave their collection to the day before you pack the SUV and head down the road.

At some point a couple of weeks before you are to be on campus for freshman orientation, you will need to start assembling and packing your "stuff" and making certain you are fully ready for your move. The farther away you have to travel, the more important this activity becomes, because your parents won't be able to head down to campus on of those early weekends with all the things you forgot.

The final getting ready period should be driven by two lists: a things-to-pack list and a tasks-to-complete list. By working on these two lists over the summer, you'll most likely manage your time and avoid any stress that packing and moving might generate. Many colleges will offer you such a list, including the things that are not permitted (e.g., halogen lighting) in your dorm room. Look for it in your orientation packet.

Unless you're heading off to a very isolated college in a very small community, you will find that a lot of the things you may need can be acquired after you get to school. Even college bookstores have many of the necessities of learning and living, although you may not find them at discount mart prices. And if you forget something personal that you need to have—the U.S. Postal Service, UPS, or FedEx will save the day.

One final summer thought—use these weeks leading up to college to read and write and engage in academic pursuits (formal summer workshops or classes, or informal Internet experiences that further prepare you for the challenges you are about to undertake. Anything you do to strengthen your skills as a future college student will pay large dividends.

Upon getting to college, be sure to participate in any orientation programs offered to you. These programs are designed to educate you about the college, its programs and services, and all of the "nuts and bolts" you need to know in order to launch a successful learning and living experience. Since orientation programs are often scheduled a few days before the campus is in full operation, they permit you to meet other students and learn about the institution in a casual and stress-free environment. Once classes start, develop your personal routine and become aware of all of the resources (people, services, etc.) positioned in various parts of the student service department. These people and programs can help you get off to and maintain a positive college experience.

## FREQUENTLY ASKED QUESTIONS

**Question:** What control do I have over the selection of my roommate and what can be done if we don't get along?
**Answer:** For most students, college represents the first real independent living experience and that includes meeting new people and learning to live in a different social environment. Roommate compatibility is created through

openness, honesty, and a willingness to understand each other's needs, likes and dislikes, habits, and other characteristics. Roommate problems occur when balance and reciprocity are missing. You can get off to the best start by completing roommate contracts and questionnaires honestly. This information will be used by housing officers in making room assignments. Attempt to resolve differences through negotiation and adjustment, not confrontation. Should you find yourself in a situation that is difficult to resolve, the college may be able to accommodate your (or your roommate's) need to move to another room.

**Question:** What is the best way to approach the college workload challenge?
**Answer:** The key to meeting college workload requirements is good time management. Begin while you are still in high school to develop these skills and make the most of the time you designate for tasks like reading, general study, research and writing assignments, and exam preparation. Identify the "time bandits" (e.g., interruptions, procrastination, telephone calls) and determine ways of avoiding or dealing with them. Have the tools and resources necessary to do your work nearby or go to the location (e.g., library, computer center) where they are available. Try creating a time budget or schedule. Determine in advance how long a task will take and stick to it. Over time, discipline and experience will produce the desired results.

**Question:** What resources exist at the college to help me if I experience difficulty with my studies?
**Answer:** Most colleges provide tutoring, mentoring, and related programs to help students who have difficulty meeting their academic obligations. Typically found in the office of student affairs or student development, these programs can only be useful if you don't wait too long before going for help. As soon as you recognize you're having trouble, talk with your professor to determine what he or she might recommend to get you back on track. If you require more intensive or long-term assistance, be certain to get in touch with the student affairs office.

## STUDENT EXERCISE 22.1

### Moving On: Packing for College

Following is a generic checklist of items that students have identified as necessary for their study and lifestyle needs. The list should not be considered exhaustive. Your personal needs and tast will dictate what you place on your personal list.

- *Study Items*
  - Calculator
  - Computer with printer
  - Dictionary/thesaurus/writing guide
  - Recorder and cassettes
  - Software
- *Desk Items*
  - Batteries (various sizes)
  - Bookends
  - Calendar
  - Cords (phone and electric)
  - File folders/notebooks
  - Index/note cards/sticky post notes
  - Paper
  - Pens/pencils/markers/highlighters
  - Ruler
  - Scissors
  - Stamps
  - Stapler
  - Paste/tape/glue
  - Stationery/envelopes
  - Tacks/tapes/paper clips/rubber ban /magnets
  - Tool set (small)
- *Leisure Time/Entertainment Items*
  - Address book/telephone/email dire ories
  - Camera and film
  - Playing cards/games
  - Radio/cassette player/CD player, h dset/headphones
  - Sporting equipment (e.g., bike, foc all, Frisbee, tennis racket, etc.)
  - Television
  - Earphones
- *Room Items*
  - Alarm clock

- Bedding (sheets, pillowcases, mattress cover)
- Bottle opener
- Bulletin board (small) and thumbtacks
- Clamp-on lamp (for bed reading)
- Coffeemaker
- Cordless phone/answering machine
- Desk lamp
- First aid kit/Band-Aids (assorted sizes)
- Flashlight
- Hangers
- Iron
- Laundry bag/basket and detergent
- Mirror (hand)
- Mugs, dishes, and utensils
- Pillows/cushions
- Posters, pictures, and room decorations
- Refrigerator (3.6 cubic feet or smaller)
- Sewing kit
- Towels and washcloths
- Throw rug(s)
- Trash and storage bags
- Under bed storage boxes/storage crates or boxes
- Wastebasket (extra)
- *Clothing Items*
  - Athletic wear/swimsuit
  - Bathrobe (bathroom isn't as close as home)
  - Clothing (seasonal)
  - Clothing (multiseasonal—if you won't be getting home)
  - Flip-flops or shower shoes
  - Foul weather gear
  - Special event apparel (for when jeans aren't appropriate)
- *Personal Items*
  - Hairbrush/dryer
  - Medications, pain relievers/vitamins
  - Soaps, shampoos, toiletries and grooming items
  - Toothbrush, toothpaste, floss, etc.
  - Shower caddy/bath tote/soap case
- *Miscellaneous Items*
  - Vaccination documentation
  - Backpack
  - Glasses/contacts (extra set)
  - Checkbook

- Credit card/ATM card
- Purchasing card (general merchaı ise, office supply, and/or hard-ware stores)
- Driver's license/passport/Social Sε ırity card
- Fan
- Insurance cards
- Luggage/trunk
- Plants
- Umbrella
- Battery charger
- *Items you will typically find providea*
  - Bed/mattress
  - Desk/desk chair
  - Dresser/closet
  - Phone (standard)
  - Wastebasket and recycling bin
- *Items not allowed or requiring prior  proval*
  - Appliances with open heating elen nts
  - Candles
  - Halogen lights
  - Hot plates

*Chapter 23*

# Parents and the High School to College Transition

The period of time when students are considering their college options and making decisions about the future is filled with excitement, discovery, and sometimes a feeling of being overwhelmed. There is much to be learned and many tasks to complete. Like all of the schooling experiences that preceded it, this is a time for parental support and involvement.

Parental participation can ensure that the student engages in effective exploration and carries out the planning and application tasks in a thorough and efficient manner. Parents can help their children formulate relevant questions and analyze the information that is gathered in response. They can also lessen the anxiety and confusion that often finds its way into the college admission process.

## GENERAL EDUCATIONAL GUIDANCE

Much of the parental role during the final years of high school must be directed toward the general educational experience, making certain that the student is engaged in studies that are consistent with his or her abilities, aptitudes, interests, and accomplishments.

Parents can also help their child in the development of effective study and time management skills and make certain he or she has the tools and materials to do an effective job as a student. They must also create an atmosphere or climate that encourages curiosity and discovery and promotes reading, experimentation, and expression.

The parent should work with teachers and counselors to track the child's learning experiences and address any issues or problems that could result in the student not realizing his or her full learning potential.

## COLLEGE GUIDANCE

The second parental guidance role deals directly with the college exploration, decision making, and application process. First, parents should help their sons and daughters understand the reasons why they are going to college and aid them in the formulation of educational and career goals. This will entail the appraisal of personal abilities, aptitudes, and interests and relating what they learn about themselves to the educational and career options before them.

This is a time to respect the individuality of children and the fact that they are still growing and maturing. Parents must also respect their children's right to make decisions about their personal future. Parents must be careful to remember who is going to college and whose life is being planned.

The student who plays a major role in the decisions that affect her or his future has a greater investment in making those decisions work. It is easier to fail or have mediocre success at the decisions that others make or force upon you. Parents should recognize the difference between guiding and steering. Guiding is an opening, promoting, and supporting parental behavior. Steering is a controlling, dominating, and insulating one.

Parents can be active participants in the college exploration and admission process. They should visit campuses with their child and participate in the parent programs offered by admission offices. Supportive parents help the child acquire and evaluate the information needed to make good decisions. Parents should (1) make certain the student has been thorough in his or her search by studying the same publications, websites, and related resources; (2) review the admission and financial aid applications and offer information or guidance in their completion; (3) make certain that tasks get completed and forms are submitted on time; and (4) be a calming force when confusion and anxiety enter the picture.

## CAREER GUIDANCE

Parents in the workplace or with career experiences can be incredibly valuable sources of information for the student explorer and decision maker. Parents can provide opportunities for their sons and daughters to learn both formally (i.e., visits to the workplace, volunteer roles, etc.) and informally (i.e., chats and discussions about their occupations and careers) about the workplace.

Many educators are now calling this a time of career and college readiness, the period in the student's life when transitions are made and life preparation is planned and initiated. Schools are designing and delivering programs and services that promote self-awareness, exploration and decision-making that are targeted at both students and their parents. Participate in them.

Above all, parents need to be proud, loving, and encouraging, and help a son or daughter deal with the outcome of the quest for college admission. When this experience has ended, they'll be the parents of a college student.

## FREQUENTLY ASKED QUESTIONS

**Question:** My parents want to be involved with my college decision. How can I keep them from taking over?

**Answer:** Your parents probably want to be involved because they care about you and your future. Make sure they know about your goals and aspirations, what you want to study, and the career or careers you feel are best suited for you. Keep them informed regarding your exploration and let them know that you are on course. When parents force their way into the process and attempt to exert undue influence in the college, exploration, identification, and decision-making process, they become what the popular media refers to as "helicopter" parents, hovering very close and being more authoritative than they probably need to be.

Many parents jump into the process because they feel their son or daughter isn't accepting the responsibility. Avoid "parental takeover" by showing that you're in control.

**Question:** How is the responsibility for guiding students through the high school to college transition different when grandparents have assumed that role with their grandchildren?

**Answer:** While grandparents raising children is not new, recent trends show the number doing it has grown dramatically. According to the American Association of Retired Persons (AARP), more than 2.7 million grandparents are engaged in a direct parenting role. AARP refers to them as "grandfamilies." When grandparents play an active role in preparing their student grandchildren for college and career, the tasks that they will perform are exactly like those presented in this guidebook for parents.

In addition, grandparents may wish to contribute financial support to defray student and family costs, and a number of programs are available for them to consider when offering this type of support. A certified financial advisor is the best source of information on these programs.

# Chapter 24

# Educational Success

## *How Counselors Can Help You*

The school counselor can be one of your greatest allies during the years that you are in high school. Unfortunately, many students fail to utilize the services of the counseling staff or participate in the programs they offer in support of their education. Others wait too long to make the counselor connection.

Consider your counselor to be a specialist, a person specifically trained to help you make the most of your educational experience and plan for your future education, career, and life. Counselors work with all students, not just those who are experiencing problems or difficulty. The terms used to describe the two basic types of counseling assistance are preventative and remedial.

Preventative assistance means a counselor can assist you in the orderly progression through school and the various educational, social, and emotional situations you will encounter. Remedial assistance is offered by the counselor when you need to address problems, resolve conflicts, and focus on solutions that stand between you and your success in school and in life.

As you progress through school, you will be faced with numerous opportunities to interact with the counselor to gather information, address concerns or problems, and set goals for the future. In many ways, your specific counseling needs may be identical to those of your peers. After all, you and your classmates are experiencing the trials and joys of adolescence and young adulthood.

Some of your counseling needs, however, may be different or unique to your personal learning and living situation. Your counselor is prepared to assist you in the confidential treatment of these special concerns.

Counselor assistance can take many forms. Sometimes one-on-one interaction between the student and counselor produces the desired outcomes. In other situations, a counselor might choose to interact with a group of students. And, in other cases, the counselor may visit the classroom or conduct a special seminar to provide information that you and your fellow students

167

might require. Finally, your counselor may serve as a "middle" person, gathering information from you, your parents and your teachers and bringing everything together in a manner that works best for you and your future. Counselors are trained and prepared to help you in the ways specified below:

- Monitoring academic achievement and assisting you in the selection of courses during high school.
- Diagnosing learning difficulties and recommending corrective measures.
- Evaluating study habits and offering suggestions on how to improve them.
- Administering tests and interpreting results.
- Assisting you in the appraisal and understanding of your aptitudes, abilities, achievements, and interests.
- Counseling you regarding future education and career options and providing information that promotes exploration and leads to sound decision making.

A good counselor-student relationship is dependent upon trust, open communication, and mutual acceptance. Your counselor will guide, not steer, you toward a greater understanding and realization of your full educational potential and show you ways to strengthen your classroom performance. Don't ask or expect your counselor to make your decisions for you.

Your counselor can help you best if he or she has a good understanding of your abilities, aptitudes, interests, and achievements. Get to know your counselor early in the high school experience and return for assistance as frequently as personal needs dictate. The result can be improved academic achievement and enhanced options for your future. Make that appointment today!

*Chapter 25*

# School to College

## *Counselors as Your Allies*

As you consider educational opportunities after high school, there are a number of experts available to help you gather information, examine options, make decisions, apply for admission and financial aid, and move from high school to college. Seize every opportunity to benefit from their expertise and guidance. You won't regret it.

### SCHOOL COUNSELORS

While you're in high school, especially during the junior and senior years, counselors can perform the following functions to aid you in the school to college transition:

- Conduct individual and group counseling sessions that help you identify learning objectives, understand the mission of different colleges and universities, examine colleges that are compatible with your academic, financial, and lifestyle requirements, evaluate information and make decisions, deal with acceptance and rejection of your college application, prepare for life as a college student, and relate educational exploration and decision making to your personal career development
- Provide information (publications, videos, Internet websites, etc.) about colleges and other postsecondary education opportunities.
- Sponsor college fairs and similar events and host college representatives in an effort to expose you to quality human resources.
- Offer guidance on how to complete college applications and financial aid forms and prepare for campus visits, admission tests, and application essays.

- Send transcripts, letters of recommendation, and school profiles to colleges in support of your application.
- Offer information and assistance to parents.

## ADMISSION AND FINANCIAL AID COUNSELORS

Counselors and admission officers at the college and university level are also equipped to aid you in this very important selection and transition process. An admission officer once suggested that the women and men who work in college admission programs should be viewed as "path lighters," not "gatekeepers." This is wise advice.

Admission officers want to attract students to their institution. But they want to recruit the "right" students: individuals who will enroll, succeed, and graduate at the end of the collegiate experience. Their role is not one of prohibiting or denying, but rather of promoting access to those students with the abilities, achievements, and interests that are required to experience success at their college or university.

Any questions that you have about the college, its educational programs, student life, or the application process should be directed to the attention of an admission counselor. Don't make application until you get the answers.

Financial aid counselors and administrators have a similar mission. They work to help you understand college costs and the financial assistance that is available to you and your family. Once they have defined your level of need, they will identify all resources (e.g., grants, scholarships, loans, work-study programs) for which you may be eligible.

These college and university representatives can also guide you through the seemingly endless forms that are required to apply for admission and financial aid.

In utilizing the services of any of these counselors, be sensitive to time constraints and calendar demands. Your needs will receive maximum attention if you establish early and ongoing contact and if you don't place impossible demands on the counselor. Help your counselors help you in the school to college transition.

## FREQUENTLY ASKED QUESTIONS

**Question:** What are the rewards and risks of hiring an independent, fee-charging counselor or consultant?
**Answer:** Private counselors have a limited caseload and can offer more individualized attention than that offered by school counselors, especially if

you haven't engaged in the progressive consideration of your options, gathering information, and related admission and financial aid tasks. Expect to pay fees that may run $1,000 to $2,500 or more for these services. Like test preparation programs and scholarship services, you're encouraged to exhaust all existing programs and services before you ask your parents to get out the checkbook.

If you decide to consult with an independent counselor, first ask him or her for a list of references that you can check before you make a financial commitment. Make certain the independent counselor is reputable and don't be afraid to ask for an agreement disclosure statement that outlines the services to be provided. The Independent Educational Consultants Association (IECA) represents experienced professionals who provide college counseling. You can consult their membership directory by specialty, city and state at www.educationalconsulting.org/.

**Question:** On several occasions I've asked my counselor to recommend the best colleges for me, but she seems reluctant to do so. Why?

**Answer:** It sounds like your counselor is a believer in the theory that the student needs to be involved in the exploration and decision-making process and, thereby become responsible for his or her choices. The role of the counselor in the college guidance process is to guide, not steer, and to help you take a realistic look at educational options in light of your abilities, achievements, and future goals. Expect your counselor to be supportive and to inform, motivate, and clarify, but ultimately, you must choose the colleges to which you will apply and the college where you will enroll.

**Question:** Many fee-charging services say they can help you gain college admission and/or financial aid. Are they worth trying?

**Answer:** Before considering any private service, I recommend that the first resource you turn to is yourself. The admission and financial aid process require your personal attention. As you get involved in the process, you will find that many resources are available to you free through your counseling office, library, and the colleges themselves. The counselors in your school and in the various college admission and financial aid offices are ready to assist you. Use these resources before you turn to any fee-charging services.

## STUDENT EXERCISE 25.1

### Tracking Counseling Sessions and Follow-up Tasks

In the space below, record notes of your counseling sessions and any follow-up tasks you must perform.

| Date | Notes and Follow-up Tasks | Completed |
|------|---------------------------|-----------|
|      |                           |           |

# Chapter 26

# Learning from the Experts

## *Reflections of Veteran Deans and Directors of Admission*

To this point the reader has been exposed to college admission and financial strategies which the author has learned over a career in counseling and through observation of the school to college transition. The latter has been influenced markedly by a number of men and women who are stalwarts in the field of college admission. Their unique perspectives have been assembled from witnessing the behaviors of tens of thousands of applicants and knowing both the right way and the wrong way to navigate the exploration, decision-making and application process.

This chapter presents the reflections of four veteran admission officers that not only support the strategies presented in this guidebook, but also offer a veteran admission officer perspective. Individually and as members of the admission teams at their respective colleges, each has examined more applications for admission and financial aid than they want to remember, and each offers their personal thoughts on the "things to do" and the "things not to do." Since their "behind the scenes" perspective won't be found in very many places, you are encouraged to read and heed their messages.

## COUNSELING AND THE THREE CS

R. Russell Shunk
Former Executive Vice President and Dean of Admissions
Dickinson College, Carlisle, PA
Past President, National Association for College Admission Counseling

"Teaching admissions" was one of my favorite roles as an admission counselor—specifically "The Three Cs—Choice, Consumerism, and Careerism."

*Choice* is about the more than 4,100 colleges and universities of all academic types, locations, sizes, costs, and more. Counselors can help you research the many options and help you and your family determine the institutional qualities that are appropriate for you.

*Consumerism* refers to the marketing in recruitment from mass mailings to individually addressed emails and many media in between. Add annual rankings to the mix and you are bombarded with messages. Marketing is a legitimate part of the process, but know that colleges are putting their best image forward.

*Careerism* in this context means choosing majors or programs (therefore colleges) leading to "hot" and/or prestigious jobs. Some parents suffer from "prenatal careerism." Because they are sure their child even prior to birth is destined to become a Nobel Prize winner, they choose her or his college curriculum even before they select the perfect preschool.

At its best admissions is a developmental process. Admission officers and counselors, college and school counselors, and independent counselors are guides to your decision making. It is called "counseling" for a reason. Although there is an element of sales in recruitment, counseling professionals with whom you will interact will want you to choose the right environment to meet your educational, extracurricular, and social goals. View us as pathlighters, not gatekeepers. We hold high the torch for you to see clearly the paths ahead.

So, explore widely, do not pre-select based on price, and visit a variety of colleges to help narrow your choices. A second more in-depth visit often helps after you have been accepted. Finally, choose the college right for you. You are the person who will be there for the next four years—not anyone else—you.

## SEARCHING FOR A GREAT FIT

Sharon M. Alton
Executive Director for Undergraduate Enrollment
American University, Washington, DC
Past Member, Board of Directors, National Association
for College Admission Counseling

Choosing a college is more than choosing a school. It's choosing the place where you will learn, work, study, and yes even play for the next four years. It's a home and it has to fit.

So how can a student ensure that she/he has identified the right fit? First, remember that the choice of a college is a highly personal decision. Because it is such a personal choice, it's worth the time for students to take stock of themselves and their personal preferences and long-term goals. We are fortunate in the United States to have all types of postsecondary institutions, varying in size, setting, location, religious affiliation, and more. So, this is a time for self-reflection. Second, the search process should be approached with the seriousness it deserves. As is the case with any other major decision, research is critical. We are fortunate to live at a time when information is plentiful and accessible. Students have the benefit of the Internet, college guides, knowledgeable professional counselors, well-meaning friends, and others. Institutions provide students with a variety of methods by which students can learn about their offerings. The importance of the decision about a college warrants a serious investment of time.

Third, (or maybe this is really "2.5" as it relates back to research), don't overlook the importance of making a campus visit. It's the best way to "try a campus on for size." Take an official campus tour and information session when classes are being held, but then take the time to walk the campus without a tour guide. Talk to the students about their experience; hang out in the campus center and read a school newspaper; listen to what students are talking about. If possible, make arrangements to visit a class or do a student-hosted, overnight visit.

Fourth, remember that an important component of fit within the current economic context has to do with affordability. Along with size, setting, and the other characteristics to consider, cost is equally important. Colleges vary in "sticker price" with community colleges and public universities offering a good value for the cost. Private universities, while typically more costly, often have considerable institutional resources devoted to minimize the financial impact on families.

Oftentimes students understand the concept of a "safety school"—where one's probability of admission is high—but they should consider the idea of a "financial safety," a place that is affordable even with minimal or no financial assistance. Consider also what might be a comfortable level of student loan debt and weigh this against the choice of major.

Finally, with all of the talk of fit, remember that there is not *one* perfect college. The goal should be to identify a select number of institutions that meet your needs. Love *every* school on the list you develop. While the decisions you receive from the schools to which you apply may vary, the personal reflection, research, and additional consideration used to develop the list will ensure that you will find that great fit wherever you land.

## REFLECTIONS OF AN OLD CODGER

Steve Syverson
Former Dean of Admission
Lawrence University, Appleton, WI
Past Member, Board of Directors, National Association
for College Admission Counseling

My parents assumed that I would attend an inexpensive public university as each of them had done. We were confronting the middle-class conundrum—too affluent to qualify for need-based financial aid, but unable to comprehend paying tuition at an elite private college. When I was admitted to Pomona College, they reconciled themselves to the idea that perhaps I could attend there for two years to take advantage of the nurturing, small-school environment, and then transfer to one of the large, less-expensive public universities for my final two years.

As it turned out, both my sister and I graduated from expensive, elite private colleges. For us, and for a multitude of families every year, colleges with seemingly prohibitive price tags turn out to be achievable.

After serving as an admission officer for a fairly long time, I will blend my personal and professional experiences and pass along several reflections to you as you pursue your college search.

1. Don't initially exclude any college because of its "sticker" price. Explore all the colleges that seem to be a good match for you, regardless of price. Ultimately, the cost may be a determining factor, but with the range of need-based aid and merit scholarships currently available, you won't actually know what any particular college will cost until you have been admitted and awarded whatever aid it offers.
2. Recognize that your college education is much more than a batch of courses or bits of information that lead to a degree. Think of it, instead, as an "educational experience" that will have at least as much impact on your personal and social development as it does on your intellectual growth. The friends you make, the opportunities you pursue outside the classroom, and the new ways of thinking to which you are exposed during your college experience, will likely shape the trajectory of your life much more than the information you retain from your classes.
3. And, finally, colleges are like jeans. There are lots of them that are the right size, but some just fit better than others. That's why it's important to go "try on" the colleges that interest you—lots of them will fit, but some will fit better than others. Many colleges will offer courses and

majors in areas of interest to you, but you should seek a place where you also are excited about the other students who are there (your potential classmates); a place where you will be challenged to work up to your potential, but will not be overwhelmed; and a place that is likely to stimulate you to try some things you've never tried before and view the world through some new lenses. There isn't just one right college—there are lots of them. So, visit campuses and leave yourself enough time to wander around and chat with some students who are not part of your official visit schedule. See if you can picture yourself there with them, and whether it is a happy picture.

Oh, there is a fourth point that needs to be made. Enjoy the process! It can be a great opportunity to learn more about yourself—what really excites you (or not) about particular campus environments, and what that tells you about your future directions. The quality of your college experience will depend more on what you put into it than on where you are doing it."

## DISPELLING SOME OF THE MYTHS
## ABOUT COLLEGE ADMISSION

Daniel J. Saracino
Former Vice Provost for Enrollment and Admission
University of Notre Dame, South Bend, IN
Past President of the National Association of College Admission Counseling

After forty-plus years of detailed involvement in the college admission process, I continue to be amazed at the misinformation that is passed from generation to generation among parents of college-bound students and their teenagers. Following are a few of those myths:

A parent announcing to all within earshot, "I loved my four years at XXX college and my child will as well." The problem here is that colleges change over the years and the qualities and characteristics that endeared the alumni to their alma mater may no longer exist. Further, the academic and nonacademic goals and interests held by the parent and child may be completely different.

*I have never heard of this college: therefore, it can't be any good.* Thousands of colleges and universities call the United States home and the average college graduate today is hard-pressed to name one hundred of them. So I challenge high school students to be open in learning about other colleges and not just focus on the few colleges that have taken on a "halo effect" because you have some familiarity with them and react to other colleges that don't have those same qualities.

*The senior year doesn't matter in the* pplication process. The college admissions committees want to know if yo are continuing to challenge yourself academically. And, while many stude s are admitted without their final senior-year transcript, they will be remin d by the college that their acceptance is contingent upon continued high vel performance in their senior year. In fact, there are now some studie that one's senior-year academic schedule and grades are a better predictor one's success in the first year of collegiate studies than earlier work.

*The SAT/ACT is the most important pa* of an applicant's file. While the test is required at many selective univer ties, the applicant's high school study as evidenced by its academic rigor, llowed by the student's grades in those courses are more important than the est score. But I would be remiss if I didn't admit that in a thorough admiss ns evaluation at highly selective colleges, everything that is in the applicat n file is important (i.e., extracurricular activities, personal statement and l ers of recommendation).

Over the years I have heard many arents and students state that "Investigating colleges is an unpleasant deal." It doesn't have to be this way. Thanks to the Internet, colleges are t your fingertips. You can go to their specific website, take a virtual tour, nd even visit with a current student. And if you are fortunate enough to n ke a personal visit to the college, your "hands-on" experience will help you nd answers to questions that just aren't addressed in the literature, websites, irtual programs, and other media. That visit can also be a great sharing oppo unity for the student and parents, including a bonding of everyone about ex ctations and direction.

I could go on and on with other myths t t continue year after year. Suffice it to say that this is an exciting time for th the student and parents. Time spent during the entire application process an help to ensure that the student is an excellent match for the college. And is not at all uncommon that the student will enroll in a college that wasn't ven on his or her "top ten list" as a high school junior.

There you have it—four veterans of the c lege admission and financial aid world offering their personal slant on what o do, what not to do, and presenting their ideas about the best ways to na gate the school to college move. Uniformly, each offers valuable insights to the strategies you must make happen in order to light your personal path o college.

## Chapter 27

# Some Closing Words about Expectations

The key to successful college decision making is effective exploration. Take a long look at yourself, your aptitudes, abilities, interests, preferences, and past achievements. Set realistic educational goals and then mount the most thorough examination of options you can orchestrate.

The philosophy of this book is that there are multiple colleges that are "right" for you and your search should be focused on identifying as many of them as possible. That will not always mean your first choice or the one your parents want you to attend. It won't likely be the one your best friend has selected. It means a college that is good for you and a lot of dynamics will interplay as the discovery runs its course.

The changes reflected in this edition of the *Bound-for-College Guidebook* include the routine adjustments that colleges, universities and the entire postsecondary education structure have made to the high school to college transition. Readers should also be aware that the continuing fallout from the coronavirus pandemic and Varsity Blues Admission Scandal needs to be monitored during the coming times. School counselors and admission officers and counselors stand ready to assist.

You get to choose what colleges to examine and the ones to which you will direct applications. The colleges, on the other hand, get to look at your academic qualifications, life experiences, and personal characteristics and determine if they match those established for future students. Then you get to sift through offers of admission and determine the best college for you. It is a very dynamic process.

A few words about expectations are appropriate here. Expect to work hard during the entire exploration and decision-making process. Expect to work even harder when you begin to apply to colleges and universities, especially when the number of applications you submit is three or greater. The same challenges will face you when you apply for scholarships and other forms of financial aid.

Expect the colleges to be interested in ou. The more "admissible" you are, —the more interest they will show in ou. In other words, the more you mirror the profile of the student they wa on their campus, the more they will do to court you and try to get you to roll. Finally, expect to be treated in a fair and ethical manner and complain hen you feel this is not the case.

Will everything be clear and make sen as you navigate the exploration, decision-making and application processe Probably not, but don't hesitate to speak up and ask for clarification whe faced with this type of situation. Counselors are positioned at various poin on the path to college to provide this kind of assistance. Remember their ro is to light paths, not lock gates.

Don't expect colleges where you don't it the profile to be as interested. They will be courteous, but clear in their v w that you don't possess the aca- demic and personal qualifications they se . And don't expect them to bend just because it is you.

Don't expect the admission formula th colleges use to remain the same from year to year. The admission recipe i redients will likely be constant, but the emphasis may shift as colleges se to create the student body they want to have. Finally, don't expect to kno the "why" about how you were accepted for enrollment or denied admiss n. Some things about this whole process will be a total mystery and de explanation. The best that you can hope for is that you and your applic ion will get a full and unbiased examination.

Hopefully the *Bound-for-College Guia* ook, with all of its information and exercises will light the path to a nun er of colleges that will help you achieve your educational and career ambi ns. Those are the colleges where you should submit applications. At the e of this exciting and sometimes tedious process, you will be in a good plac —most likely the right place. You will be a college student.

# Index

academic fit, 11–12

academic philosophy. *See* college search

academic record. *See* admission criteria

accommodations. *See* college search

Accrediting Commission of Career Schools and Colleges (ACCSC), 38, 115

achievements. *See* self and personal assessment

ACT and ACT Assessment. *See* admission testing

admissibility, 6, 13, 110

admissibility quotient (AQ), 6

admission application: appearance, 123; application checklist, 126–127; application fees, 124; application list, 118–120; Coalition Application, 121; Common Application and Common App Online, 22, 68, 121, 123–124, 126; Common Black College Application, 121

admission competition: competitive colleges, 6–8, 96; determining selectivity, 66; examining the competition, 116; open admission colleges, 96; selective colleges, 3–5, 53, 95, 97–98, 116, 178

admission counselors, admission officers, and financial aid counselors,

1–3, 5, 7, 44, 53, 59, 62, 74, 77, 96, 98, 100, 110, 114–115, 123–125, 136, 170, 173–174, 179

admission criteria: achievement in college preparatory studies, 1, 100, 102; class rank, 1–2, 5, 100; essays and writing samples, 2, 23, 69, 99–100; 105–107, 121–124, 126, 141, 169; extracurricular activities, 2, 6, 19, 100–101; grade point average (GPA) and grades, 1, 100, 124, 140–141; interview, 3, 43, 77, 81, 84–86, 100, 105, 107, 113, 122, 124, 126; new admission assessments, 3; service learning, 2, 118; special talents and characteristics, 3, 137; teacher and counselor recommendations, 2, 23, 100, 122, 124–125; test scores, 1–2, 4, 19–20, 43, 54, 100, 102–103, 106, 116, 122, 124, 126; volunteering and volunteerism, 2, 40; work-study and work experience, 6, 140

admission decision. *See* admission process

admission denied. *See* admission process

admission myths. *See* admission process

admission offers. *See* admission process

# About the Author

**Dr. Frank Burtnett** is a veteran counselor, teacher, student service administrator, education association officer, and consultant who currently serves as president of Education Now, an educational consulting, research, and resource development firm located in Springfield, Virginia, and Rockport, Maine. Over his career, Frank served as the executive director of the National Association for College Admission Counseling (NACAC) and associate executive director of the American Counseling Association (ACA).

Frank is the author of *The Bound-for-Career Guidebook*, a companion publication for students in the Rowman & Littlefield Education library. His *Career Challenges: Straight Talk about the Steps and Missteps of Career Development* is a Rowman & Littlefield title appropriate for readers of all ages.

Frank serves as an adjunct professor on the counselor education faculty of the College of Health and Education, Department of Counseling at Marymount University in Arlington, Virginia. He has also developed and presented seminars on educational and career development topics for numerous institutions, agencies, organizations, and private sector sponsors. He is also a popular speaker at both professional and public programs.

Frank holds a Bachelor of Science degree in education from Shippensburg University (Pennsylvania) and Master of Arts and Doctor of Education degrees in counseling from George Washington University (Washington, D.C.) and has earned the National Certified Counselor and National Certified Career Counselor credentials of the National Board for Certified Counselors. He is a registered counselor (RC2478) in the state of Maine.